Ch

Italian ...ebook

Debora Mazza

Donald Watt

Chambers

First published by Chambers Harrap Publishers Ltd 2006
7 Hopetoun Crescent
Edinburgh EH7 4AY

ISBN 0550 10283 3

Editor & Project Manager
Anna Stevenson

Publishing Manager
Patrick White

Prepress
Susan Lawrie

Designed and typeset by Chambers Harrap Publishers Ltd, Edinburgh
Printed and bound by Tien Wah Press (PTE.) LTD., Singapore
Illustrations by Art Explosion

CONTENTS

Introduction	4
Pronunciation and alphabet	5
Everyday conversation	7
Getting to know people	14
Travelling	22
Accommodation	33
Eating and drinking	41
Food and drink	49
Going out	57
Tourism and sightseeing	64
Sports and games	69
Shopping	76
Photos	85
Banks	88
Post offices	90
Internet cafés and e-mail	92
Telephone	94
Health	99
Problems and emergencies	106
Time and date	110
Numbers	117
English-Italian dictionary	119
Italian-English dictionary	150
Grammar	180
Holidays and festivals	186
Useful addresses	188
Conversion tables	190

INTRODUCTION

This brand new English-Italian phrasebook from Chambers is ideal for anyone wishing to try out their foreign language skills while travelling abroad. The information is practical and clearly presented, helping you to overcome the language barrier and mix with the locals.

Each section features a list of useful words and a selection of common phrases: some of these you will read or hear, while others will help you to express yourself. The simple phonetic transcription system, specifically designed for English speakers, ensures that you will always make yourself understood.

The book also includes a mini bilingual dictionary of around 4,000 words, so that more adventurous users can build on the basic structures and engage in more complex conversations.

Concise information on local culture and customs is provided, along with practical tips to save you time. After all, you're on holiday – time to relax and enjoy yourself! There is also a food and drink glossary to help you make sense of menus, and ensure that you don't miss out on any of the national or regional specialities.

Remember that any effort you make will be appreciated. So don't be shy – have a go!

ABBREVIATIONS USED IN THIS GUIDE

adj	adjective
adv	adverb
conj	conjunction
f	feminine noun
fpl	feminine plural noun
m	masculine noun
mpl	masculine plural noun
n	noun
prep	preposition
v	verb

PRONUNCIATION

You will find the pronunciation for every Italian word or phrase given in this book shown after it in italics. By reading out this phonetic transcription, you will be able to make yourself understood to an Italian. Always put the stress on the vowels or syllables that appear in bold: this is very important in Italian!

The Italian alphabet consists of 21 letters. They are pronounced as follows :

a *a*	**h** *akka*	**q** *koo*
b *bee*	**i** *ee*	**r** *erray*
c *chee*	**l** *ellay*	**s** *essay*
d *dee*	**m** *emmay*	**t** *tee*
e *ay*	**n** *ennay*	**u** *oo*
f *effay*	**o** *o*	**v** *voo*
g *jee*	**p** *pee*	**z** *dzeta*

You sometimes find the letters **j** (*ee loonga*), **k** (*kappa*), **w** (*doppee-a voo*), **x** (*eeks*) and **y** (*eepseelon*) in words of foreign origin.

When **c** and **g** come before **a**, **o** or **u**, they have a hard sound:

> casa *kaza*   gallina *galleena*
> coltello *koltelo*   lago *lago*
> curare *kuraray*   gusto *goosto*

When they come before **e** or **i**, **c** is pronounced *ch* and **g** is pronounced *j*:

> celebre *chelaybray*   gente *jentay*
> cinema *cheenayma*   girasole *jeerasolay*

When there is an **i** between the consonants **c** or **g** and the vowels **a**, **o**, or **u**, they are also pronounced *ch* and *j*:

> ciao *cha-o*   cioccolata *chokkolata*
> ciuffo *chooffo*   giornata *jornata*

When there is an **h** between the consonants **c** or **g** and the vowels **e** and **i**, they are pronounced with a hard sound:

> anche *ankay*   chitarra *keetarra*
> spaghetti *spaghettee*   ghiottone *ghee-ottonay*

Sca, sco, scu, schi, sche are pronounced *ska, sko, skoo, skee, skay*:

> scatola *skatola*　　　　schiaffo *skee-affo*
> scoprire *skopreeray*　　schermo *skermo*
> scultura *skooltoora*

Sce and **sci** are pronounced *shay* and *shee*:

> scena *shayna*　　　　scimmia *sheemee-a*

Gli is pronounced *ly* as in the English word 'mi**lli**on':

> moglie *molyay*

Z is pronounced as *dz* in some words and as *ts* in others:

> zio *dzee-o*　　　　　pizza *peetsa*

Between two vowels **s** is pronounced *z*; everywhere else, it is pronounced *s* :

> casa *caza*　sono *sono*　cassa *kassa*

E has a weak and a strong pronunciation: the weak form is pronounced *e* as in the English word 'g**e**t' and the strong form is pronounced *ay* as in the English word 'd**ay**':

> petto *petto*　　　　　nero *nayro*

Au is pronounced *ow* as in the English word 'n**ow**':

> auto *owto*

EVERYDAY CONVERSATION

Italians usually greet each other with a handshake.

There are two ways to say "you" in Italian: the informal **tu** and the formal **lei**, which is conjugated like the third person singular. As a rule of thumb, if you would address someone using their first name, use **tu** in Italian; if you do not know their name or would address them by Mr, Mrs etc in English, use **lei**. **Dare del tu** means to use **tu** when talking to someone because you are on familiar terms with them and **dare del lei** means to use **lei** when talking to someone because you do not know them or are on formal terms with them. Most of the time in Italian, you do not need to use the actual words **tu** or **lei** when you are talking to someone because the form of the verb itself makes this clear.

Note that the informal word **ciao**, which is used both when you meet someone and when you are leaving, corresponds to "hi" or "hello" and "bye" or "see you" in English.

The basics

bye	ciao *chow*
excuse me	mi scusi *mee skoozee*
good afternoon	buongiorno *boo-onjorno*
goodbye	arrivederci *arreevayderchee*
good evening	buonasera *boo-onasayra*
good morning	buongiorno *boo-onjorno*
goodnight	buonanotte *boo-onanottay*
hello	ciao *chow*
hi	ciao *chow*
no	no *no*
OK	va bene *va baynay*
pardon	(mi) scusi *(mee) skoozee*
please	per favore *per favoray*

thanks, thank you	grazie *gratsee-ay*
yes	sì *see*

Expressing yourself

I'd like ...
vorrei ...
voray-ee ...

we'd like ...
vorremmo ...
voraymo ...

do you want ...?
vuole ...?
voo-olay ...?

do you have ...?
ha ...?
a ...?

is there ...?
c'è ...?
chay ...?

are there ...?
ci sono ...?
chee sono ...?

how ...?
come ...?
comay ...?

why ...?
perché ...?
perkay ...?

when ...?
quando ...?
kwando ...?

what ...?
cosa ...?
koza ...?

where is ...?
dov'è ...?
dovay ...?

where are ...?
dove sono ...?
dovay sono ...?

how much is it?
quanto costa?
kwanto costa?

what is it?
che cos'è?
kay kozay?

do you speak English?
parla inglese?
parla eenglayzay?

where are the toilets, please?
dov'è la toilette, per favore?
dovay la twalet, per favoray?

how are you?
come stai?
comay sta-ee?

fine, thanks
bene, grazie
baynay, gratsee-ay

thanks very much
grazie mille
gratsee-ay meelay

no, thanks
no, grazie
no, gratsee-ay

yes, please
sì, grazie
see, gratsee-ay

you're welcome
prego
praygo

see you later
ci vediamo
chee vaydee-amo

I'm sorry
mi dispiace
mee deespee-achay

Understanding

aperto	open
attenzione	attention
divieto di sosta	no parking
fuori servizio	out of order
ingresso	entrance
libero	free
prenotato	reserved
toilette	toilets
uscita	exit
vietato …	do not …
vietato fumare	no smoking

c'è/ci sono …
there's/there are …

benvenuto
welcome

le dispiace se …?
do you mind if …?

si accomodi
please take a seat

un attimo, per favore
one moment, please

PROBLEMS UNDERSTANDING ITALIAN

Expressing yourself

pardon?
(mi) scusi?
(mee) skoozee?

what?
come?
comay?

could you repeat that, please?
potrebbe ripetere, per favore?
potrebbay reepetayray, per favoray?

could you speak more slowly?
potrebbe parlare più lentamente?
potrebbay parlaray pyoo lentamentay?

I don't understand
non capisco
non kapeesko

I understand a little Italian
capisco un po' d'italiano
kapeesko oon po deetalee-ano

I can understand Italian but I can't speak it
capisco l'italiano ma non lo parlo
kapeesko leetalee-ano ma non lo parlo

I speak hardly any Italian
parlo pochissimo l'italiano
parlo pokeeseemo leetalee-ano

do you speak English?
parla inglese?
parla eenglayzay?

how do you say ... in Italian?
come si dice ... in italiano?
komay see deechay ... een eetalee-ano?

how do you spell it?
come si scrive?
komay see skreevay?

could you write it down for me?
me lo potrebbe scrivere?
may lo potrebbay skreevayray?

what's that called in Italian?
come si chiama quello in italiano?
comay see kee-ama kwello een eetalee-ano?

Understanding

capisce l'italiano?
do you understand Italian?

glielo scrivo
I'll write it down for you

vuol dire ...
it means ...

è una specie di ...
it's a kind of ...

SPEAKING ABOUT THE LANGUAGE

Expressing yourself

I learned a few words from my phrasebook
ho imparato qualche parola da un manuale di conversazione
o eemparato kwalkay parola da oon manoo-alay dee konversatsee-onay

I did it at school but I've forgotten everything
l'ho studiato a scuola, ma ho dimenticato tutto
lo stoodee-ato a skoo-ola, ma o deementeekato tooto

I can just about get by
me la cavo più o meno
may la kavo pyoo o mayno

I hardly know two words!
so a malapena un paio di parole!
so a malapayna oon pa-ee-o dee parolay

I find Italian a difficult language
trovo che l'italiano sia una lingua difficile
trovo kay leetalee-ano see-a oona leengwa deefeecheelay

I know the basics but no more than that
ho solo qualche nozione di base, niente di più
o solo kwalkay notsee-onay dee bazay, nee-entay dee pyoo

people speak too quickly for me
la gente parla troppo in fretta per me
la gentay parla tropo een fretta per may

Understanding

ha un buon accento
you have a good accent

parla benissimo l'italiano
you speak very good Italian

ASKING THE WAY

Expressing yourself

excuse me, can you tell me where … is, please?
mi scusi, mi può dire dov'è …, per favore?
mee skoosee, mee poo-o deeray dovay …, per favoray?

which way is it to …?
da che parte è …?
da kay partay ay …?

is there a … near here?
c'è un/una … qui vicino?
chay oon/oona … kwee veecheeno?

can you tell me how to get to …?
mi può dire come si va a …?
mee poo-o deeray comay see va a …?

could you show me on the map?
me lo potrebbe far vedere sulla cartina?
may lo potrebbay far vaydayray soola karteena?

is there a map of the town somewhere?
c'è una pianta della città da qualche parte?
chay oona pee-anta della cheeta da kwalkay partay?

is it far?
è lontano?
ay lontano?

I'm looking for …
sto cercando …
sto cherkando …

I'm lost
mi sono perso
mee sono perso

Understanding

destra	right
girare	to turn
proseguire	to keep going
salire	go up
scendere	to go down
seguire	to follow
sempre dritto	straight ahead
sinistra	left

è a cinque minuti da qui in macchina
it's five minutes away by car

è la prima/seconda/terza a sinistra
it's the first/second/third on the left

all'incrocio, giri a destra
turn right at the junction

alla banca, giri a sinistra
turn left at the bank

prenda la prossima uscita
take the next exit

non è lontano
it's not far

è a piedi?
are you on foot?

è a due passi
it's just round the corner

GETTING TO KNOW PEOPLE

The basics

bad	cattivo *katteevo*
beautiful	bello *bello*
boring	noioso *noy-ozo*
cheap	economico *aykonomeeko*
expensive	caro *karo*
good	buono *boo-ono*
great	fantastico *fantasteeko*
interesting	interessante *eentayressantay*
nice	bello *bello*
not bad	niente male *nee-entay malay*
well	bene *baynay*
to hate	detestare *daytestaray*
to love	adorare *adoraray*

INTRODUCING YOURSELF AND FINDING OUT ABOUT OTHER PEOPLE

Expressing yourself

my name's …
mi chiamo …
mee kee-amo …

what's your name?
come ti chiami?
comay tee kee-amee?

how do you do!
molto lieto!
molto lee-ayto!

pleased to meet you!
(molto) piacere!
(molto) pee-achayray!

this is my husband
questo è mio marito
kwesto ay mee-o mareeto

this is my partner, Karen
questa è la mia compagna, Karen
kwesta ay la mee-a companya, Karen

I'm English
sono inglese
sono eenglayzay

we're Welsh
siamo gallesi
see-amo gallayzee

where are you from?
di dove sei?
dee dovay say-ee?

I'm from ...
sono di ...
sono dee ...

how old are you?
quanti anni hai?
kwantee annee a-ee?

I'm 22
ho ventidue anni
o venteedoo-ay annee

what do you do for a living?
cosa fai nella vita?
koza fa-ee nella veeta?

are you a student?
sei studente?
say-ee stoodentay?

I work
lavoro
lavoro

I'm studying law
studio diritto
stoodee-o deereeto

I'm a teacher
sono insegnante
sono eensaynyantay

I work in marketing
lavoro nel marketing
lavoro nel marketing

I'm retired
sono in pensione
sono een pensee-onay

I'm self-employed
lavoro in proprio
lavoro een propree-o

I have two children
ho due figli
o doo-ay feelyee

we don't have any children
non abbiamo figli
non abbee-amo feelyee

I work part-time
lavoro part-time
lavoro par-ta-eem

two boys and a girl
due maschi e una femmina
doo-ay maskee ay oona femmeena

I stay at home with the children
non lavoro e mi occupo dei miei figli
non lavoro ay mee okupo day-ee mee-ay-ee feelyee

a boy of five and a girl of two
un bambino di cinque anni e una bambina di due
oon bambeeno dee cheenkway annee ay oona bambeena dee doo-ay

have you ever been to Britain?
sei mai stato in Gran Bretagna?
say-ee ma-ee stato een gran bretanya?

Understanding

è inglese?
are you English?

conosco l'Inghilterra piuttosto bene
I know England quite well

anche noi siamo qui in vacanza
we're on holiday here too

mi piacerebbe molto andare in Scozia prima o poi
I'd love to go to Scotland one day

TALKING ABOUT YOUR STAY

Expressing yourself

I'm here on business
sono qui per lavoro
sono kwee per lavoro

we're on holiday
siamo in vacanza
see-amo een vakantsa

I arrived three days ago
sono arrivato tre giorni fa
sono areevato tray jornee fa

we've been here for a week
siamo qui da una settimana
see-amo kwee da oona setteemana

I'm only here for a few days
mi fermo solo qualche giorno
mee fermo solo kwalkay jorno

we're just passing through
siamo solo di passaggio
see-amo solo dee passajo

this is our first time in Italy
è la prima volta che veniamo in Italia
ay la preema volta kay venee-amo een eetalee-a

we're here to celebrate our wedding anniversary
siamo venuti per festeggiare il nostro anniversario di matrimonio
see-amo vaynootee per festejaray eel nostro anneeversaree-o dee matreemonee-o

we're on our honeymoon
siamo in viaggio di nozze
see-amo een vee-ajo dee notsay

we're here with friends
siamo venuti con degli amici
see-amo vaynootee kon delyee ammeechee

we're touring around Umbria
stiamo facendo un giro dell'Umbria
stee-amo fachendo oon jeero del oombree-a

we managed to get a cheap flight
siamo riusciti a trovare un volo economico
see-amo ree-oosheetee a trovaray oon volo aykonomeeko

we're thinking about buying a house here
stiamo considerando l'idea di comprare una casa qui
stee-amo konseedayrando leeday-a dee kompraray oona caza kwee

Understanding

buona permanenza!
enjoy your stay!

quanto si ferma?
how long are you staying?

buon proseguimento della vacanza!
enjoy the rest of your holiday!

è la prima volta che viene in Italia?
is this your first time in Italy?

le piace qui?
do you like it here?

è stato a …?
have you been to …?

STAYING IN TOUCH

Expressing yourself

we should stay in touch
dovremmo tenerci in contatto
dovraymo tenayrchee een kontato

I'll give you my e-mail address
ti do il mio indirizzo e-mail
tee do eel mee-o eendeereetso ee-mayl

here's my address, if you ever come to Britain
questo è il mio indirizzo, caso mai ti capitasse di venire in Gran
 Bretagna
*kwesto ay eel mee-o eendeereetso, kazo ma-ee tee kapeetassay dee
 vayneeray een gran bretanya*

Understanding

mi dai il tuo indirizzo?   **hai un indirizzo e-mail?**
will you give me your address?   do you have an e-mail address?

sei sempre il benvenuto qui da noi
you're always welcome to come and stay with us here

EXPRESSING YOUR OPINION

Expressing yourself

I really like ...
mi piace molto ...
mee pee-achay molto ...

I really liked ...
mi è piaciuto molto ...
mee ay pee-achooto molto ...

I don't like ...
non mi piace ...
non mee pee-achay ...

I didn't like ...
non mi è piaciuto ...
non mee ay pee-achooto ...

I love ...
mi piace moltissimo ...
mee pee-achay molteesseemo ...

I loved ...
mi è piaciuto moltissimo ...
mee ay pee-achooto molteesseemo ...

I would like ...
mi piacerebbe ...
mee pee-achayrebbay ...

I would have liked ...
mi sarebbe piaciuto ...
mee sarebbay pee-achooto ...

I find it ...
lo trovo ...
lo trovo ...

I found it ...
l'ho trovato ...
lo trovato ...

it's lovely
è bellissimo
ay belleesseemo

it was lovely
è stato bellissimo
ay stato belleesseemo

I agree
sono d'accordo
sono dakordo

I don't agree
non sono d'accordo
non sono dakordo

I don't know
non lo so
non lo so

I don't mind
per me, è lo stesso
per may, ay lo stesso

it really annoys me
mi dà veramente fastidio
mee da vayramentay fasteedee-o

it was boring
era noioso
ayra noy-ozo

it's a rip-off
è un furto
ay un foorto

it gets very busy at night
c'è molta gente di sera
chay molta gentay dee sayra

it's too busy
c'è troppa gente
chay troppa gentay

it's very quiet
c'è pochissima gente
chay pokeesseema gentay

I really enjoyed myself
mi sono divertito molto
mee sono deeverteeto molto

we had a great time
ci siamo divertiti da matti
chee see-amo deeverteetee da mattee

it sounds interesting
sembra interessante
sembra eentayressantay

I don't like the sound of it
non mi sembra una buona idea
non mee sembra oona boo-ona eeday-a

there was a really good atmosphere
c'era una bellissima atmosfera
chayra oona belleesseema atmosfayra

we met some nice people
abbiamo incontrato delle persone simpatiche
abbee-amo eenkontrato dellay personay seempatteekay

we found a great hotel
abbiamo trovato un albergo fantastico
abbee-amo trovato oon albergo fantasteeko

Understanding

ti piace …?
do you like …?

vi siete divertiti?
did you enjoy yourselves?

dovresti andare a …
you should go to …

ti consiglio …
I recommend …

è una zona molto bella
it's a lovely area

non ci sono troppi turisti
there aren't too many tourists

non è bello come si dice
it's a bit overrated

non andare nel fine settimana, c'è troppa gente
don't go at the weekend: it's too busy

TALKING ABOUT THE WEATHER

Expressing yourself

have you seen the weather forecast for tomorrow?
hai visto le previsioni del tempo per domani?
a-ee veesto lay prayveezee-onee del tempo per domannee?

it's going to be nice
farà bello
fara bello

it isn't going to be nice
farà brutto
fara bruto

it's really hot
fa veramente caldo
fa vayramentay caldo

it gets cold at night
di notte, fa freddo
dee nottay, fa fredo

the weather was beautiful
il tempo è stato bello
eel tempo ay stato bello

it rained a few times
è piovuto qualche volta
ay pee-ovooto kwalkay volta

there was a thunderstorm
c'è stato un temporale
chay stato oon temporalay

it's very humid here
è molto umido qui
ay molto oomeedo kwee

20

it's been lovely all week
il tempo è stato bellissimo tutta la settimana
eel tempo ay stato belleesseemo toota la setteemana

we've been lucky with the weather
siamo stati fortunati con il tempo
see-amo stattee fortoonattee kon eel tempo

Understanding

dovrebbe piovere
it's supposed to rain

è previsto bel tempo per il resto della settimana
they've forecast good weather for the rest of the week

domani farà di nuovo molto caldo
it will be hot again tomorrow

si muore di caldo
it's sweltering

fa un caldo incredible
it's boiling hot

si gela
it's freezing

c'è un tempo da cani
the weather's terrible

sto gelando
I'm freezing

piove a dirotto
it's pouring down

TRAVELLING

The basics

airport	aeroporto *a-ayroporto*
boarding	imbarco *eembarko*
boarding card	carta d'imbarco *karta deembarko*
boat	nave *navay*
bus	autobus *owtoboos*
bus station	stazione degli autobus *statsee-onay delyee owtoboos*
bus stop	fermata dell'autobus *fermata del owtoboos*
car	macchina *makeena*
check-in	check-in *chekeen*
coach	pullman *poolman*
ferry	traghetto *tragheto*
flight	volo *volo*
gate	uscita *oosheeta*
left-luggage (office)	deposito bagagli *daypozeeto bagalyee*
luggage	bagagli *bagalyee*
map	carta *karta*
motorway	autostrada *owtostrada*
passport	passaporto *passaporto*
plane	aereo *a-ayray-o*
platform	binario *beenaree-o*
railway station	stazione (ferroviaria) *statsee-onay (ferovee-aree-a)*
return (ticket)	(biglietto di) andata e ritorno *(beelyetto dee) andata ay reetorno*
road	strada *strada*
shuttle bus	navetta *navetta*
single (ticket)	(biglietto di) sola andata *(beelyetto dee) sola andata*
street	via *vee-a*
streetmap	pianta *pee-anta*
taxi	taxi *taksee*
terminal	terminale *termeenalay*
ticket	biglietto *beelyetto*
timetable	orari *oraree*

town centre	centro *chentro*
train	treno *trayno*
tram	tram *tram*
underground	metropolitana *metropoleetana*
underground station	stazione della metropolitana *statsee-onay della metropoleetana*
to book	prenotare *praynotaray*
to hire	noleggiare *nolejaray*

Expressing yourself

where can I buy tickets?
dove si comprano i biglietti?
dovay see comprano ee beelyettee

a ticket to ..., please
un biglietto per ..., per favore
oon beelyetto per ..., per favoray

how much is a ticket to ...?
quanto costa un biglietto per ...?
kwanto kosta oon beelyetto per ...?

I'd like to book a ticket
vorrei fare una prenotazione
voray-ee faray oona praynotatsee-onay

is there an earlier/later one?
ce n'è uno prima/dopo?
chay nay oono preema/dopo?

how long does the journey take?
quanto dura il viaggio?
kwanto doora eel vee-ajo?

are there any concessions for students?
ci sono sconti per gli studenti?
chee sono skontee per lyee stoodentee

could I have a timetable, please?
potrei avere un prospetto con gli orari, per favore?
potray-ee avayray oon prospetto kon lyee oraree, per favoray?

is this seat free?
è libero questo posto?
ay leebayro kwesto posto?

I'm sorry, there's someone sitting there
mi dispiace, questo posto è occupato
mee deespee-achay, kwesto posto ay okoopato

Understanding

annullato	cancelled
arrivi	arrivals
biglietti	tickets
coincidenze	connections
donne	ladies
entrata	entrance
informazioni	information
ingresso vietato	no entry
partenze	departures
ritardato	delayed
toilette	toilets
uomini	gents
uscita	exit

non ci sono più posti
everything is fully booked

BY PLANE

The national airline is Alitalia, which, like British Airways, operates scheduled flights to and from the major Italian cities. There are also various budget airlines that operate flights mostly within Italy and Europe.

Ticket prices are most expensive in the high season, from June to September, and cheapest from November to March, apart from at Christmas.

Expressing yourself

where's the British Airways check-in?
dov'è il banco del check-in della British Airways?
dovay eel banko del chekeen della breeteesh ayrwayz?

I've got an e-ticket
ho un biglietto elettronico
o oon beelyetto ayletroneeko

what time do we board?
a che ora è l'imbarco?
a kay ora ay leembarko?

one suitcase and one piece of hand luggage
una valigia e un bagaglio a mano
oona valeeja ay oon bagalyo a mano

I'd like to confirm my return flight
vorrei confermare il volo di ritorno
voray-ee konfermaray eel volo dee reetorno

one of my suitcases is missing
una delle mie valigie è stata smarrita
oona dellay mee-ay valeejay ay stata zmareeta

my luggage hasn't arrived
i miei bagagli non sono arrivati
ee mee-ay-ee bagalyee non sono areevatee

the plane was two hours late
l'aereo aveva due ore di ritardo
la-ayray-o avayva doo-ay oray dee reetardo

I've missed my connection
ho perso la coincidenza
o perso la ko-eencheedentsa

I've left something on the plane
ho dimenticato qualcosa sull'aereo
o deementeekato kwalkoza soola-ayray-o

I want to report the loss of my luggage
vorrei fare una denuncia di smarrimento bagagli
voray-ee faray oona daynooncha dee zmareemento bagalyee

Understanding

controllo passaporti	passport control
dogana	customs

imbarco immediato	immediate boarding
merci da dichiarare	goods to declare
niente da dichiarare	nothing to declare
ritiro bagagli	baggage reclaim
sala d'imbarco	departure lounge
voli nazionali	domestic flights

attenda in sala d'imbarco
please wait in the departure lounge

preferisce un posto lato finestrino o corridoio?
would you like a window seat or an aisle seat?

deve cambiare a …
you'll have to change in …

quanti bagagli ha?
how many bags do you have?

qualcuno le ha dato degli oggetti da portare a bordo?
has anyone given you anything to take on board?

i suoi bagagli superano il limite consentito di cinque chili
your luggage is five kilos overweight

ecco la sua carta d'imbarco
here's your boarding card

ha preparato lei le sue valigie?
did you pack all your bags yourself?

l'imbarco inizia alle …
boarding will begin at …

ultima chiamata per …
this is a final call for …

si accomodi pure all'uscita numero …
please proceed to gate number …

può chiamare questo numero per verificare se i suoi bagagli sono arrivati
you can call this number to check that your luggage has arrived

BY TRAIN, COACH, BUS, UNDERGROUND, TRAM

In towns, you are most likely to get around by bus or tram. Rome, Milan, Naples and Genoa have underground systems, but the networks are not very extensive. The Rome underground has only two lines and trains stop running at 11.30pm (12.30am on Saturdays). Tickets can be bought at counters, from machines or in tobacconists. They are valid for all forms of public transport. In Rome, a single ticket costs less than a euro and is valid for 75 minutes. You can also buy one-day or weekly passes. In Milan, you can buy a book of single tickets or a pass for one or two days.

Trains are cheaper than in the UK and the rail network is very extensive. The main rail company is Trenitalia, the state company. You can buy passes for periods of between four and ten days. It is advisable to book a seat before travelling. Children under four travel free and children from four to 12 travel half-price. Always punch your ticket in the machine at the platform entrance to validate it before you get on the train or you could face a fine.

Expressing yourself

can I have a map of the underground, please?
posso avere una piantina della metropolitana?
posso avayray oona pee-anteena della metropoleetana?

what time is the next train to ...?
a che ora è il prossimo treno per ...?
a kay ora ay eel prosseemo trayno per ...?

which platform is it for ...?
da che binario parte il treno per ...?
da kay beenaree-o partay eel trayno per ...?

which line do I take to get to ...?
che linea si deve prendere per andare a ...?
kay leenay-a see devay prenderay per andaray a ...?

is this where the coach leaves for …?
è da qui che parte il pullman per …?
ay da kwee kay partay eel poolman per …?

can you tell me when I need to get off?
mi può dire quando devo scendere?
mee poo-o deeray kwando devo shenderay?

what time is the last train?
a che ora è l'ultimo treno?
a kay ora ay loolteemo trayno?

where can I catch a bus to …?
dove si prende l'autobus per …?
dovay see prenday lowtoboos per …?

is this the stop for …?
è questa la fermata per …?
ay kwesta la fermata per …?

I've missed my train/bus
ho perso il treno/l'autobus
o perso eel trayno/lowtoboos

Understanding

accesso ai treni	to the trains
biglietteria	ticket office
biglietto giornaliero	one-day travel card
mensile	monthly
prenotazioni	bookings
settimanale	weekly

c'è una fermata un po' più avanti a destra
there's a stop a bit further along on the right

deve prendere l'autobus numero …
you need to get the number … bus

solo denaro contato
exact money only, please

deve cambiare a …
you'll have to change at …

questo treno ferma a …
this train calls at …

tra due fermate
two stops from here

BY CAR

Everyone knows that Venice is a pedestrianized city. If you visit on a day trip, you can park in the **Piazzale Roma** car park just before you get to the island. If you are planning a longer stay, you should leave your car in the **Tronchetto** car park, which is signposted on the road into Venice. You will then be taken into town by boat. In some cities, the city centre is closed to all traffic except residents during the day.

Italy has a good network of motorways, most of which are run by the state company Autostrade S.p.A. Tolls are payable on all motorways. Always keep the ticket you get when you join the motorway network, because if you do not show it at the tollbooth when leaving the motorway, you will have to pay the maximum rate.

Hitchhiking is allowed, except on motorways, but is not very common in Italy.

Taxis are more expensive than in the UK. There are taxi ranks at rail and bus stations, or you can book one by phone. You cannot hail one in the street, because it is illegal for them to stop to pick you up.

Expressing yourself

where can I find a service station?
dove posso trovare una stazione di servizio?
dovay posso trovaray oona statsee-onay dee serveetsee-o?

fill it up, please
il pieno, per favore
eel pee-ayno, per favoray

how much is it per litre?
quanto costa al litro?
kwanto kosta al leetro?

we got stuck in a traffic jam
siamo rimasti bloccati nel traffico
see-amo reemastee blokatee nel trafeeko

the battery's dead
la batteria è scarica
la batteree-a ay skareeka

is there a garage near here?
c'è un'officina nei paraggi?
chay oonofeecheena nay-ee parajee?

I've broken down
sono rimasto in panne
sono reemasto een pannay

we've run out of petrol
siamo rimasti senza benzina
see-amo reemastee sentsa bendzeena

I've lost my car keys
ho perso le chiavi della macchina
o perso lay kee-avee della makeena

I've got a puncture and my spare tyre is flat
ho bucato e ho la ruota di scorta a terra
o bookato ay o la roo-ota dee skorta a terra

we've just had an accident
abbiamo appena avuto un incidente
abbee-amo apayna avooto oon eencheedentay

how long will it take to repair?
quanto tempo ci vorrà per la riparazione?
kwanto tempo chee vora per la reeparatsee-onay?

can you help us to push the car?
ci può aiutare a spingere la macchina?
chee poo-o a-yootaray a speengeray la makeena?

Hiring a car

I'd like to hire a car for a week
vorrei noleggiare una macchina per una settimana
voray-ee nolejaray oona makeena per oona setteemana

an automatic (car)
una macchina con il cambio automatico
oona makeena kon eel kambee-o owtomateeko

I'd like to take out comprehensive insurance
vorrei una polizza kasko
voray-ee oona poleetsa kasko

Getting a taxi

is there a taxi rank near here?
c'è un posteggio dei taxi nei paraggi?
chay oon postejo day-ee taksee nay-ee parajee?

I'd like to go to ...
vorrei andare a ...
voray-ee andaray a ...

you can drop me off here, thanks
può lasciarmi qui, grazie
poo-o lasharmee kwee, gratsee-ay

I'd like to book a taxi for 8pm
vorrei prenotare un taxi per le otto di stasera
voray-ee praynotaray oon taksee per lay otto dee stasayra

how much will it be to go to the airport?
quanto mi verrebbe a costare fino all'aeroporto?
kwanto mee verrebbay a kostaray feeno ala-ayroporto?

Hitchhiking

I'm going to ...
vado a ...
vado a ...

can you drop me off here?
può lasciarmi qui?
poo-o lasharmee kwee?

thanks for the lift
grazie del passaggio
gratsee-ay del passajo

we hitched a lift
abbiamo fatto l'autostop
abbee-amo fato lowtostop

could you take me as far as ...?
mi potrebbe portare fino a ...
mee potrebbay portaray feeno a ...?

Understanding

altre direzioni other directions
autonoleggio car hire
completo full *(car park)*
conservare lo scontrino keep your ticket
divieto di sosta no parking
parcheggio car park
posti (macchina) spaces *(car park)*
rallentare slow

sosta a pagamento pay parking
tutte le direzioni all directions

mi servono la sua patente, un documento di identità, un giustificativo di domicilio e la carta di credito
I'll need your driving licence, another form of ID, proof of address and your credit card

deve versare una cauzione di 300 euro
there's a 300-euro deposit

d'accordo, salga; la porto fino a ...
all right, get in; I'll take you as far as …

BY BOAT

The main destinations for ferries are Greece, Bosnia, Corsica and, of course, Sicily and Sardinia. There are frequent departures (particularly in summer) from Genoa, Livorno, Civitavecchia, Pescara, Bari, Naples and Venice. In Venice, the only form of public transport is the **vaporetto** (boat-bus).

Expressing yourself

how long is the crossing? **I'm seasick**
quanto dura la traversata? ho il mal di mare
kwanto doora la traversata? *o eel mal dee maray*

Understanding

passeggeri senza veicolo foot passengers only
prossima partenza alle ... next crossing at …

ACCOMMODATION

A hotel is called either **hotel** or **albergo**. A **pensione** is a guesthouse and is usually family-run and cheaper than a hotel. You can make bookings either from the UK or on arrival. Prices vary according to the season: they are more expensive in July and August, and around Christmas and Easter. Breakfast is normally included in the room price. Some hotels offer half board (**mezza pensione**) or full board (**pensione completa**).

Camping is only permitted on licensed campsites. These are called **campeggi** and vary in the facilities offered, but many are equipped with restaurants, bars, supermarkets, swimming pools etc.

Youth hostels are called **ostelli della gioventù**. You will need a Youth Hostels Association or Hostelling International membership card to use these, which you should get before your trip.

If you want a holiday in the country that offers the opportunity to sample traditional Italian country life and cooking, you could stay at an **agriturismo**. These range from simple farms to luxury country hotels with a wide range of facilities.

The basics

bath	vasca (da bagno) *vaska (da banyo)*
bathroom	(stanza da) bagno *(stantsa) da banyo*
bathroom with shower	bagno con doccia *banyo kon docha*
bed	letto *letto*
bed and breakfast	bed and breakfast *bed and brekfast*
cable television	tv via cavo *teevoo vee-a cavo*
campsite	campeggio *kampejo*
caravan	roulotte *roolot*
cottage	casetta di campagna *kazetta dee campanya*
double bed	letto matrimoniale *letto matreemonee-alay*
double room	camera doppia *kamayra doppee-a*
family room	camera per famiglie *kamayra per fameelyee-ay*

flat	appartamento *apartamento*
full-board	pensione completa *pensee-onay complayta*
fully inclusive	tutto compreso *tooto komprayzo*
half-board	mezza pensione *medza pensee-onay*
hotel	albergo *albergo*
key	chiave *kee-avay*
rent	affitto *affeeto*
room with an en-suite bathroom	camera con bagno *kamayra kon banyo*
self-catering accommodation	residence *rezeedens*
shower	doccia *docha*
single bed	letto singolo *letto seengolo*
single room	camera singola *kamayra seengola*
tenant	inquilino *eenkweeleeno*
tent	tenda *tenda*
toilet	gabinetto *gabbeenetto*
youth hostel	ostello (della gioventù) *ostello (della joventoo)*
to book	prenotare *praynotaray*
to rent	affittare *affeetaray*
to reserve	prenotare *praynotaray*

Expressing yourself

I have a reservation
ho una prenotazione
o oona praynotatsee-onay

the name's ...
il nome è ...
eel nomay ay ...

do you take credit cards?
accettate le carte di credito?
achetatay lay kartay dee craydeeto?

Understanding

camere libere	vacancies
completo	full
privato	private
reception	reception
toilette	toilets

34

posso vedere il suo passaporto, per favore?
could I see your passport, please?

può compilare questa scheda?
could you fill in this form?

HOTELS

Expressing yourself

do you have any vacancies?
avete delle camere libere?
avaytay dellay kamayray leebayray?

how much is a double room per night?
quanto costa a notte una camera doppia?
kwanto kosta a nottay oona kamayra doppee-a?

I'd like to reserve a double room/a single room
vorrei prenotare una camera doppia/una camera singola
voray-ee praynotaray oona kamayra doppee-a/oona kamayra seengola

for three nights
per tre notti
per tray nottee

is breakfast included?
la colazione è compresa?
la colatsee-onay ay komprayza?

would it be possible to stay an extra night?
è possibile rimanere ancora una notte?
ay posseebeelay reemanayray ankora oona nottay?

do you have any rooms available for tonight?
avete delle camere libere per stanotte?
avaytay dellay kamayray leebayray per stanottay?

do you have any family rooms?
avete delle camere per famiglie?
avaytay dellay kamayray per fameelyee-ay?

would it be possible to add an extra bed?
è possibile aggiungere un letto supplementare?
ay posseebeelay ajoonjayray oon letto sooplaymentaray?

could I see the room first?
potrei vedere la camera prima?
potray-ee vaydayray la kamayra preema?

do you have anything bigger/quieter?
non avete qualcosa di più grande/di più calmo?
non avaytay kwalkoza dee pyoo granday/dee pyoo calmo?

that's fine, I'll take it
va bene, la prendo
va baynay, la prendo

is there a lift?
c'è un ascensore?
chay oon ashensoray?

could you recommend any other hotels?
mi potrebbe raccomandare qualche altro albergo?
mee potrebbay rakomandaray kwalkay altro albergo?

what time do you serve breakfast?
a che ora è servita la colazione?
a kay ora ay serveeta la colatsee-onay?

is the hotel near the centre of town?
l'albergo è vicino al centro?
lalbergo ay veecheeno al chentro?

what time will the room be ready?
a che ora sarà pronta la camera?
a kay ora sara pronta la kamayra?

the key for room ..., please
la chiave della camera ..., per favore
la kee-avay della kamayra ..., per favoray

could I have an extra blanket?
potrei avere una coperta in più?
potray-ee avayray oona coperta een pyoo?

the air conditioning isn't working
l'aria condizionata non funziona
laree-a kondeetsee-onata non foontsee-ona

Understanding

mi dispiace, siamo al completo
I'm sorry, but we're full

ci è rimasta solo una camera singola
we only have a single room available

per quante notti?
how many nights is it for?

qual è il suo nome?
what's your name, please?

le camere sono disponibili a partire da mezzogiorno
check-in is from midday

deve lasciare la camera entro le undici
you have to check out before 11am

la prima colazione è servita nel ristorante dalle sette e trenta alle nove
breakfast is served in the restaurant between 7:30 and 9:00

desidera avere un quotidiano al mattino?
would you like a newspaper in the morning?

la sua camera non è ancora pronta
your room isn't ready yet

può lasciare qui i suoi bagagli
you can leave your bags here

YOUTH HOSTELS

Expressing yourself

do you have space for two people for tonight?
avete posto per due persone per stanotte?
avaytay posto per doo-ay personay per stanottay?

we've booked two beds for three nights
abbiamo prenotato due posti letto per tre notti
abbee-amo praynotato doo-ay postee letto per tray nottee

could I leave my backpack at reception?
posso lasciare lo zaino alla reception?
posso lasharay lo dza-eeno alla raysepshon?

do you have somewhere we could leave our bikes?
c'è un posto dove possiamo lasciare le bici?
chay oon posto dovay possee-amo lasharay lay beechee?

I'll come back for it around 7 o'clock
vengo a riprenderlo verso le sette
vengo a reeprenderlo verso lay settay

there's no hot water
non c'è acqua calda
non chay akwa calda

the sink's blocked
il lavandino è otturato
eel lavandeeno ay ottoorato

Understanding

le lenzuola sono fornite
bed linen is provided

ha la tessera di socio?
do you have a membership card?

l'ostello riapre alle sei
the hostel reopens at 6 pm

SELF-CATERING

Expressing yourself

we're looking for somewhere to rent near a town
cerchiamo qualcosa da affittare nelle vicinanze di una città
cherkee-amo kwalkoza da affeetaray nellay veecheenantsay dee oona cheeta

where do we pick up/leave the keys?
dove dobbiamo prendere/lasciare le chiavi?
dovay dobee-amo prenderay/lashary lay kee-avee?

is electricity included in the price?
l'elettricità è compresa nel prezzo?
layletreecheeta ay komprayza nel pretso?

are bed linen and towels provided?
lenzuola e asciugamani sono forniti?
lentsoo-ola ay ashoogamannee sono forneetee?

is a car necessary?
ci vuole la macchina?
chee voo-olay la makeena?

is there a pool?
c'è la piscina?
chay la peesheena?

is the accommodation suitable for elderly people?
è una sistemazione adatta a persone anziane?
ay oona seestaymatsee-onay adatta a personay antseeanay?

where is the nearest supermarket?
dove si trova il supermercato più vicino?
dovay see trova eel soopermerkato pyoo veecheeno?

Understanding

si prega di lasciare la casa pulita e in ordine
please leave the house clean and tidy after you leave

la casa è interamente ammobiliata
the house is fully furnished

è tutto compreso nel prezzo
everything is included in the price

la macchina è indispensabile in questa zona
you really need a car in this part of the country

CAMPING

Expressing yourself

is there a campsite near here?
c'è un campeggio qui vicino?
chay oon kampejo kwee veecheeno?

I'd like to book a space for a two-person tent for three nights
vorrei prenotare un posto per una tenda da due per tre notti
voray-ee praynotaray oon posto per oona tenda da doo-ay per tray nottee

how much is it a night?
qual è la tariffa giornaliera?
kwal ay la tareefa jornalee-ayra?

where is the shower block?
dove sono le docce?
dovay sono le dochay?

can we pay, please? we were at space …
possiamo pagare? eravamo al posto numero …
possee-amo pagaray? ayravamo al posto noomayro …

Understanding

costa … a persona al giorno
it's … per person per night

se le serve qualcosa, mi chieda pure
if you need anything, just come and ask

EATING AND DRINKING

There are various types of restaurant in Italy. The most general word is **ristorante**, which can be any type of restaurant. The **trattoria**, which is usually a small, family-run concern, offers a fairly restricted choice of simple traditional meals. The **osteria** can range from a simple restaurant resembling a trattoria to a high-class establishment offering sophisticated local dishes and a very good and expensive wine list. Pizzerias are, of course, a very common and cheaper alternative and are a favourite with Italians. Fast-food outlets can be found in all Italian cities nowadays, and more exotic restaurants are becoming increasingly common, but only in big cities.

If you order water in a restaurant you will usually be served mineral water. You should always specify whether you want still (**naturale** or **non gasata**) or sparkling (**frizzante** or **gasata**). Alternatively, you can ask for a jug of tap water (**acqua in caraffa**). Service is rarely included, and there may be an additional cover charge (**coperto**).

For a quick snack on the go, most bars, cafés and sandwich shops sell slices of pizza, **panini** (sandwiches) and **toast** (toasted sandwiches).

For a drink, you can go to a bar, a club, or an **enoteca** (wine bar). **Birrerie** (pubs), which are usually open from 6 or 7pm until late, offer a wide range of beers as well as sandwiches and pasta dishes and are very popular with young people. Tea rooms are normally cake shops (**pasticcerie**) with a few tables, and a bar where you can eat and drink standing up. Italians often go to a bar for breakfast, which typically consists of coffee and a croissant (**caffè con brioche**).

The basics

beer	birra *beera*
bill	conto *konto*
black coffee	caffè (nero) *kaffay (nayro)*
bottle	bottiglia *boteelya*
bread	pane *pannay*

41

breakfast	(prima) colazione *(preema) kolatsee-onay*
coffee	caffè *kaffay*
Coke®	Coca-Cola® *koka-kola*
dessert	dolce *dolchay*
dinner	cena *chayna*
first course	primo *preemo*
fruit juice	succo di frutta *sooko dee froota*
lemonade	gazzosa *gadzoza*
lunch	pranzo *prandzo*
main course	secondo *saykondo*
menu	menu *maynoo*
mineral water	acqua minerale *akwa meenayralay*
red wine	vino rosso *veeno rosso*
rosé wine	vino rosato *veeno rozato*
salad	insalata *eensalata*
sandwich	panino *panneeno*
service	servizio *serveetsee-o*
sparkling	*(water, wine)* frizzante *freedzantay*
starter	antipasto *anteepasto*
still	*(water)* naturale *natooralay*
tea	tè *tay*
tip	mancia *mancha*
water	acqua *akwa*
white coffee	caffellatte *kaffaylattay*
white wine	vino bianco *veeno bee-anko*
wine list	carta dei vini *karta day-ee veenee*
wine	vino *veeno*
to eat	mangiare *manjaray*
to have breakfast	fare colazione *faray kolatsee-onay*
to have dinner	cenare *chaynaray*
to have lunch	pranzare *prandzaray*
to order	ordinare *ordeenaray*

Expressing yourself

shall we go and have something to eat?
andiamo a mangiare qualcosa?
andee-amo a manjaray kwalkoza?

do you want to go for a drink?
vuoi andare a bere qualcosa?
voo-o-ee andaray a bayray kwalkoza?

can you recommend a good restaurant?
mi può consigliare un buon ristorante?
mee poo-o konseelyaray oon boo-on reestorantay?

I'm not very hungry
non ho molta fame
non o molta famay

excuse me! (to call the waiter)
scusi!
skoozee!

cheers!
cincin!
cheencheen!

that was lovely
era squisito
ayra skweezeeto

could you bring us an ashtray, please?
ci può portare un posacenere, per favore?
chee poo-o portaray oon pozachaynayray, per favoray?

where are the toilets, please?
dov'è la toilette, per favore?
dovay la twalet, per favoray?

Understanding

da portar via   takeaway
sul posto   eating in

mi dispiace, non serviamo più dopo le undici
I'm sorry, we stop serving at 11pm

RESERVING A TABLE

Expressing yourself

I'd like to reserve a table for tomorrow evening
vorrei prenotare un tavolo per domani sera
voray-ee praynotaray oon tavolo per domannee sayra

for two people
per due (persone)
per doo-ay (personay)

around 8 o'clock
intorno alle otto
eentorno allay otto

do you have a table available any earlier than that?
non avreste un tavolo libero prima?
non avrestay oon tavolo leebayro preema?

I've reserved a table – the name's …
ho prenotato un tavolo - il nome è …
o praynotato oon tavolo - eel nomay ay …

Understanding

prenotato
reserved

per che ora?
for what time?

per quante persone?
for how many people?

a che nome?
what's the name?

fumatori o non fumatori?
smoking or non-smoking?

avete una prenotazione?
do you have a reservation?

vi va bene il tavolo nell'angolo?
is this table in the corner OK for you?

mi dispiace, ma al momento non ci sono tavoli liberi
I'm afraid we're full at the moment

ORDERING FOOD

Expressing yourself

I'd like …
vorrei …
voray-ee …

yes, we're ready to order
sì, abbiamo scelto
see, abbee-amo shelto

no, could you give us a few more minutes?
no, ci può lasciare ancora qualche minuto?
no, chee poo-o lasharay ankora kwalkay meenooto?

could I have ...?
potrei avere ...?
potray-ee avayray ...?

I'll have that
prendo questo
prendo kwesto

I'm not sure, what's "tagliatelle alla boscaiola"?
non lo so; cosa sono le "tagliatelle alla boscaiola"?
non lo so; koza sono le "talyee-atellay alla boska-ee-ola"?

some water, please
dell'acqua, per favore
dellakwa, per favoray

does it come with vegetables?
è servito con un contorno?
ay serveeto kon oon kontorno?

what are today's specials?
quali sono i piatti del giorno?
kwallee sono ee pee-attee del jorno?

what desserts do you have?
che dolci avete?
kay dolchee avaytay?

that's for me
quello è per me
kwello ay per may

a bottle of red/white wine
una bottiglia di vino rosso/bianco
oona boteelya de veeno rosso/bee-anko

this isn't what I ordered: I wanted ...
non è quello che ho ordinato: volevo ...
non ay kwello kay o ordeenato: volayvo ...

could we have some more bread, please?
potremmo avere altro pane, per favore?
potraymo avayray altro pannay, per favoray?

could you bring us another jug of water, please?
ci potrebbe portare un'altra caraffa d'acqua, per favore?
chee potrebbay portaray oonaltra karafa dakwa, per favoray?

Understanding

avete scelto?
are you ready to order?

ritorno tra poco
I'll come back in a few minutes

(andava) tutto bene?
was everything OK?

mi dispiace, non ci sono più ...
I'm sorry, we don't have any... left

cosa prendete da bere?
what would you like to drink?

prendete un dolce o il caffè?
would you like dessert or coffee?

EATING AND DRINKING

BARS AND CAFÉS

(i)

If you ask for a coffee (**un caffè**) in Italy, what you will get is an **espresso**, which is a small strong black coffee. If you prefer your coffee milky, ask for a **caffellatte**, although Italians normally only drink this at breakfast time. The same is true for the **cappuccino**: coffee topped with frothy steamed milk and sprinkled with chocolate powder. Alternatively you could have a **caffè con panna**, a coffee topped with whipped cream. A **macchiato** is an espresso with a dash of milk, while a **latte macchiato** is just the opposite: a glass of steamed milk topped with a dash of coffee. If you want a liqueur coffee, ask for a **caffè corretto**. If you don't like coffee at all, the hot chocolate (**cioccolata**) is excellent and usually very rich. Different regions have their own spirits and liqueurs, and many drinks are made using Campari or Aperol (a dark, orange-flavoured liqueur). Small glasses of wine are always popular. Bars usually offer a few nibbles, such as crackers, crisps or olives, to go with your drink.

Expressing yourself

I'd like…
vorrei …
voray-ee …

a Coke®/a diet Coke®
una Coca-Cola®/una Coca-Cola® light
oona koka-kola/oona koka-kola la-eet

a glass of white/red wine
un bicchiere di vino bianco/rosso
oon beekee-ayray dee veeno bee-anko/rosso

a black coffee
un caffè (nero)
oon kaffay (nayro)

a white coffee
un caffellatte
oon kaffaylattay

a cup of tea
un tè
oon tay

a coffee and a croissant
un caffè con brioche
oon kaffay kon bree-osh

a cup of hot chocolate
una cioccolata calda
oona chokolata kalda

the same again, please
un altro, per favore
oon altro, per favoray

Understanding

analcolico
non-alcoholic

cosa prende?
what would you like?

questa è l'area non fumatori
this is the non-smoking area

le dispiacerebbe pagare ora, per favore?
could I ask you to pay now, please?

> **Some informal expressions**
>
> **alzare il gomito** to drink too much
> **essere sbronzo** to be plastered
> **essere pieno** to be full
> **strafogarsi** to stuff oneself

THE BILL

Expressing yourself

the bill, please
il conto, per favore
eel konto, per favoray

how much do I owe you?
quanto fa?
kwanto fa?

is service included?
il servizio è compreso?
eel serveetsee-o ay komprayzo?

do you take credit cards?
accettate le carte di credito?
achettatay lay kartay dee craydeeto?

EATING AND DRINKING

I think there's a mistake in the bill
penso che ci sia un errore nel conto
penso kay chee see-a oon erroray nel konto

Understanding

pagate insieme?
are you all paying together?

sì, il servizio è compreso
yes, service is included

FOOD AND DRINK

A classic Italian meal consists of a starter (**antipasto**), a first course (**primo** – a pasta dish, risotto or soup), a main course (**secondo** – meat or fish with salad or vegetables), and a dessert. You often need to order side dishes (**contorni**) for the main dish separately. You do not, however, have to order all four courses. Service (**servizio**) and cover charge (**coperto**) are usually added to the bill. Most restaurants, especially in tourist centres, offer special menus for lunch which are usually cheaper.

Understanding

a fette	sliced
affumicato	smoked
al cartoccio	in foil
al forno	*(pasta)* baked; *(chicken)* roast
alla griglia	grilled
al sangue	rare
ben cotto	well done
bollito	boiled
brasato	braised
cotto al forno a legna	cooked in a wood-fired oven
dorato	golden brown
essiccato	dried
freddo	cold
fresco	fresh
fritto	fried
impanato	in breadcrumbs
in carpione	soused
in purè	puréed
lesso	boiled
piccante	hot, spicy
ripieno	stuffed
saltato	sauté
sciolto	melted

stufato	stewed

antipasti starters

bruschetta	slice of toasted bread rubbed with garlic and olive oil
calamari fritti	fried squid
caponata	Sicilian dish of fried aubergines, celery, olives, and capers
carpaccio	thin slices of raw meat with olive oil and shavings of Parmesan cheese
insalata russa	Russian salad
mozzarella in carrozza	mozzarella sandwich dipped in egg and fried
prosciutto e melone	Parma ham and melon
salumi	cold meats
sottaceti	pickled vegetables

primi piatti first courses

agnolotti	ravioli
lasagne al forno	lasagne
minestra	soup
minestrone	minestrone
pappardelle al sugo	wide pasta strips with a meat sauce
pasta	pasta
pasta e fagioli	pasta and bean soup
penne all'arrabbiata	short pasta tubes with a spicy tomato sauce
polenta	dish made from maize flour
risi e bisi	rice and peas
riso	rice
risotto alla marinara	seafood risotto
risotto alla milanese	risotto with saffron
spaghetti all'amatriciana	spaghetti with a tomato and bacon sauce
spaghetti alla puttanesca	spaghetti with a tomato, anchovy, black olive and caper sauce
spaghetti alle vongole	spaghetti with clams
spaghetti al pomodoro	spaghetti with a tomato sauce

tagliatelle alla carbonara	tagliatelle with an egg yolk, bacon, and Parmesan cheese sauce
tortellini alla boscaiola	type of ravioli with a mushroom filling
trenette	long flat pasta pieces
zuppa di pesce	fish soup

secondi piatti main courses

abbacchio	spring lamb
agnello al forno	roast lamb
bistecca ai ferri	grilled steak
bistecca alla fiorentina	T-bone steak
cacciagione	game
carne	meat
cozze alla marinara	mussels in white wine
fegato alla veneziana	liver and onions
frutti di mare	seafood
pesce	fish
pollo arrosto	roast chicken
saltimbocca alla romana	piece of veal rolled up with ham and sage
scaloppine alla milanese	escalopes in breadcrumbs
sogliola alla mugnaia	sole meunière
vitello tonnato	cold veal with a tuna mayonnaise

contorni side dishes

carciofi alla romana	artichokes with parsley, mint, and garlic
fagiolini al burro	green beans with butter
insalata verde/mista	green/mixed salad
melanzane alla parmigiana	baked aubergines in a tomato sauce, topped with Parmesan cheese
patate fritte	chips
verdura cotta	cooked vegetables

formaggio cheese

| **caprino** | goat's cheese |

fontina	full-fat sweet cheese from Valle d'Aosta
gorgonzola	gorgonzola
mozzarella di bufala	buffalo mozzarella
pecorino	sheep's milk cheese
provolone	Southern Italian hard cheese
ricotta	unsalted soft white sheep's milk cheese
scamorza	soft, often smoked cheese
stracchino	soft fresh cheese from Lombardy
taleggio	soft mature cheese from Lombardy

pizze pizzas

calzone	folded-over pizza
pizza margherita	mozzarella, basil and tomato pizza
pizza napoletana	mozzarella, basil, tomato and anchovy pizza
pizza quattro stagioni	four seasons pizza

frutta e dolci fruit and desserts

affogato al caffè	ice cream with coffee poured over it
budino al cioccolato	chocolate pudding
cassata	ice cream with chocolate, candied fruit and cream
cassata (siciliana)	ricotta cheese, chocolate and candied fruit gateau
crostata	tart
crostata di fragole	strawberry tart
frutta di stagione	fruit in season
gelato	ice cream
macedonia	fruit salad
panna cotta	cold dessert made by heating cream with sugar and gelatine
tiramisù	sponge fingers soaked in coffee and topped with cream cheese and chocolate
torta	cake
torta di mele	apple pie
zabaione	dessert made from egg yolks, sugar, and Marsala
zuppa inglese	trifle

FOOD GLOSSARY

acciuga anchovy
aceto vinegar
acqua minerale gassata sparkling mineral water
acqua minerale naturale still mineral water
acquavite grappa
aglio garlic
ala di pollo chicken wing
albicocca apricot
alcolici alcohol
amaro bitters
analcolico non-alcoholic
ananas pineapple
anatra duck
anguilla eel
anguria watermelon
aperitivo aperitif
aragosta spiny lobster
asparagi asparagus
astice lobster
banana banana
basilico basil
besciamella béchamel sauce
bevande drinks
bibite soft drinks
bicchiere glass
birra beer
biscotto biscuit
bresaola dried salt beef
broccoli broccoli
brodo broth
bue beef
burro butter
cacciagione game
caffè coffee

caffè corretto coffee laced with alcohol
caffè lungo weak coffee
caffè macchiato coffee with a dash of milk
caffè ristretto strong coffee
caffellatte white coffee
cannelloni cannelloni
cantuccini hard almond biscuits
capesante scallops
cappelletti type of ravioli
capperi capers
cappone capon
capra goat
capriolo venison
caramelle sweets
carciofo artichoke
carota carrot
carpa carp
castagna chestnut
cavallo horse
cavolfiore cauliflower
cavolo cabbage
cece chickpea
cervo venison
cetriolino gherkin
cetriolo cucumber
cibo food
ciliegia cherry
cinghiale wild boar
cioccolata hot chocolate
cioccolatino chocolate
cioccolato *(food)* chocolate
cipolla onion
colomba pasquale dove-shaped Easter cake

coltello knife
condimento dressing; seasoning; sauce
coniglio rabbit
cono gelato ice-cream cone
contorno side dish
coppa cured neck of pork
coppa gelato ice cream
cornetto croissant; ice-cream cone
coscia di pollo chicken leg
cotechino large pork sausage
cotoletta cutlet
cozza mussel
cucchiaino teaspoon
cucchiaio spoon
dattero date
digestivo liqueur
fagiano pheasant
fagiolino green bean
fagiolo bean
faraona guinea fowl
fegato liver
fetta biscottata rusk
fetta slice
fettuccine ribbon-shaped pasta
fico fig
finocchio fennel
focaccia flat bread made with olive oil
fonduta fondue
fragola strawberry
frappè milk shake
frittata omelette
frizzante sparkling
gallina hen
gamberetto shrimp
gambero prawn

gamberone king prawn
gazzosa lemonade
gnocchetti sardi small shell shaped pasta pieces
gnocchi alla romana semolina dumplings topped with cheese and baked
gnocchi di patate potato dumplings
granchio crab
granita water ice
grattugiato grated
grissini breadsticks
in umido stewed
involtini stuffed rolls of meat
lampone raspberry
lenticchia lentil
lepre hare
limoncello lemon liqueur
liquore liqueur
luccio pike
maiale pork
maionese mayonnaise
mandarino mandarin
mandorla almond
manzo beef
margarina margarine
marmellata jam, marmalade
mela apple
melone melon
menta mint
meringa meringue
merluzzo cod
mirtillo blueberry
mora blackberry
mortadella large sausage served sliced
moscato muscat

mucca cow
nasello hake
nocciola hazelnut
nocciolina peanut
noce walnut
olio oil
oliva olive
orata sea bream
ostrica oyster
pagnotta loaf
pancetta bacon
pancetta affumicata smoked
  bacon
pandoro sponge cake eaten at
  Christmas
pane bread
panettone loaf containing sultanas
  and candied fruit eaten at
  Christmas
panforte flat cake containing
  candied fruit and nuts
panino roll
panna cream
panna montata whipped cream
parmigiano Parmesan cheese
pastasciutta pasta
pasta fresca fresh pasta
pasticcini cakes
patata potato
patatine crisps
pecora sheep
pepe pepper *(seasoning)*
peperonata peppers, tomatoes
  and onions cooked in oil
peperone pepper *(vegetable)*
pera pear
pernice partridge
pesca peach

pesce fish
pescespada swordfish
pesto basil, garlic, pecorino
  cheese, pine nut and olive oil sauce
petto di pollo breast of chicken
pinoli pine nuts
piselli peas
pollo chicken
polpette meatballs
polpo octopus
pomodoro tomato
porcini cep mushrooms
porro leek
posate cutlery
prezzemolo parsley
prosciutto cotto cooked ham
prosciutto crudo cured ham
prugna plum
quaglia quail
ravanello radish
ribes currant
rosmarino rosemary
rosticceria shop or restaurant
  selling roast meats
rucola rocket
salame salami
salatini crackers
sale salt
salmone salmon
salsa verde parsley, anchovy,
  garlic, caper and olive oil sauce
salsiccia sausage
salvia sage
sardina sardine
scampo langoustine
sedano celery
semifreddo ice-cream dessert
senape mustard

seppia cuttlefish
sgombro mackerel
speck smoked ham
spezzatino stew
spiedino kebab
spinaci spinach
spremuta d'arancia freshly
  squeezed orange juice
spremuta di limone freshly
  squeezed lemon juice
spumante sparkling wine
stracciatella *(dessert)* vanilla ice
  cream with grated chocolate;
  (soup) soup with beaten egg and
  Parmesan cheese
succo di frutta fruit juice
succo di pomodoro tomato juice
sugo di pomodoro tomato sauce
tacchino turkey
tartufo truffle
tavola calda café
toast toasted ham-and-cheese
  sandwich

tonno tuna
torrone nougat
tovaglia tablecloth
tovagliolo napkin
tramezzino sandwich
trippa tripe
trota trout
uova strapazzate scrambled eggs
uovo egg
uovo sodo hard-boiled egg
uva grapes
vino bianco white wine
vino rosato rosé wine
vino rosso red wine
vongola clam
zafferano saffron
zampone pig's trotter stuffed with
  minced meat
zenzero ginger
zucca pumpkin
zucchino courgette

You can find out about cultural events in the local press. Most newspapers produce a supplement at the weekend listing national and local events.

English-language films are usually dubbed into Italian, though some cinemas do show subtitled versions. Plays are, of course, performed in Italian, though you can find some English-language performances, for example in Rome. Opera is very popular in Italy, and many cities have their own opera houses.

In summer, festivals are held all over the country. Any occasion will do: there are festivals of grapes, wild boar, chestnuts and fish, among others. A banquet is served, followed by dancing to live music.

In the evening there are, of course, all the many restaurants, bars, cafés, and clubs to choose from, but many Italians will simply go out to have a walk or an ice cream in the city centre. People tend to eat later in the south, so they go out later in the evening.

The basics

ballet	danza classica *dantsa klasseeka*
band	complesso *komplesso*
bar	bar *bar*
cinema	cinema *cheenayma*
circus	circo *cheerko*
classical music	musica classica *moozeeka klasseeka*
club	discoteca *deeskotayka*
concert	concerto *koncherto*
dubbed film	film doppiato *feelm dopee-ato*
festival	festival *festeeval*
film	film *feelm*
folk music	musica folk *moozeeka folk*
group	gruppo *groopo*
jazz	jazz *jets*

modern dance	danza moderna *dantsa moderna*
musical	musical *myoozeekal*
party	festa *festa*
play	spettacolo teatrale *spettakolo tay-atralay*
pop music	musica pop *moozeeka pop*
rock music	rock *rok*
show	spettacolo *spetakolo*
subtitled film	film sottotitolato *feelm sototeetolato*
theatre	teatro *tay-atro*
ticket	biglietto *beelyetto*
to book	prenotare *praynotaray*
to go out	uscire *oosheeray*

SUGGESTIONS AND INVITATIONS

Expressing yourself

where can we go?
dove possiamo andare?
dovay possee-amo andaray?

what do you want to do?
cosa vuoi fare?
koza voo-o-ee faray?

shall we go for a drink?
andiamo a bere qualcosa?
andee-amo a bayray kwalkoza?

what are you doing tonight?
cosa fai stasera?
koza fa-ee stasayra?

do you have plans?
hai qualcosa in programma?
a-ee kwalkoza een programa?

would you like to ...?
ti andrebbe di ... ?
tee andrebbay dee ...?

we were thinking of going to ...
stavamo pensando di andare a ...
stavamo pensando dee andaray a ...

I can't today, but maybe some other time
oggi non posso, magari un'altra volta
ojee non posso, magaree oonaltra volta

I'm not sure I can make it
non sono sicuro di potere
non sono seekooro dee potayray

I'd love to
molto volentieri
molto volentee-ayree

ARRANGING TO MEET

Expressing yourself

what time shall we meet?
a che ora ci vediamo?
a kay ora chee vaydee-amo?

where shall we meet?
dove ci troviamo?
dovay chee trovee-amo?

would it be possible to meet a bit later?
sarebbe possibile vederci un po' più tardi?
sarebbay posseebeelay vaydayrchee oon po pyoo tardee?

I have to meet … at nine
devo incontrare … alle nove
dayvo eenkontraray … allay novay

sorry I'm late
mi dispiace, sono in ritardo
mee deespee-achay, sono een reetardo

I don't know where it is but I'll find it on the map
non so dove sia, ma lo cerco sulla cartina
non so dovay see-a, ma lo cherko soola carteena

see you tomorrow night
ci vediamo domani sera
chee vaydee-amo domannee sayra

are you going to eat beforehand?
avrai già mangiato?
avra-ee ja manjato?

I'll meet you later: I have to stop by the hotel first
ci vediamo dopo: devo passare prima dall'albergo
chee vaydee-amo dopo: dayvo passaray preema dalalbergo

I'll call/text you if there's a change of plan
ti chiamo/mando un SMS se c'è un cambiamento di programma
tee kee-amo/mando oon essay-emmay-essay say chay oon kambee-amento dee programa

Understanding

ti va bene?
is that ok with you?

ci vediamo là
I'll meet you there

ti vengo a prendere intorno alle otto
I'll come and pick you up at about 8 o'clock

possiamo trovarci fuori
we can meet outside

GOING OUT

ti do il mio numero, così mi puoi chiamare domani
I'll give you my number and you can call me tomorrow

FILMS, SHOWS AND CONCERTS

Expressing yourself

is there a guide to what's on?
c'è un programma degli spettacoli?
chay oon programa delyee spetakolee?

I'd like three tickets for …
vorrei tre biglietti per …
voray-ee tray beelyettee per …

two tickets, please
due biglietti, per favore
doo-ay beelyettee, per favoray

I've seen the trailer
ho visto la presentazione
o veesto la prayzentatsee-onay

what time does it start?
a che ora comincia?
a kay ora komeencha?

I'd like to go and see a show
mi piacerebbe andare a vedere uno spettacolo
mee pee-achayrebbay andaray a vaydayray oono spetakolo

I'll find out whether there are still tickets available
mi informo per sapere se si trovano ancora dei biglietti
mee eenformo per sapayray say see trovano ancora day-ee beelyettee

do we need to book in advance?
dobbiamo prenotare in anticipo?
dobee-amo praynotaray een anteecheepo?

how long is it on for?
fino a quando lo danno?
feeno a kwando lo danno?

are there any free concerts?
ci sono concerti gratuiti?
chee sono conchertee gratoo-eetee?

are there tickets for another day?
ci sono dei biglietti per un altro giorno?
chee sono day-ee beelyettee per oon altro jorno?

I'd like to go to a bar with some live music
vorrei andare in un bar con musica dal vivo
voray-ee andaray een oon bar kon moozeeka dal veevo

what sort of music is it?
che genere di musica è?
kay jenayray dee moozeeka ay?

Understanding

biglietteria	box office
cinema d'essai	arthouse cinema
prenotazioni	bookings
sugli schermi dal …	on general release from …
superproduzione	blockbuster

è un concerto all'aperto
it's an open-air concert

esce la settimana prossima
it comes out next week

ha avuto delle ottime recensioni
it's had very good reviews

lo danno alle otto all'Odeon
it's on at 8pm at the Odeon

non ci sono più posti per questo spettacolo
that showing's sold out

è tutto esaurito fino al …
it's all booked up until …

non c'è bisogno di prenotare in anticipo
there's no need to book in advance

la rappresentazione dura due ore e mezza compreso l'intervallo
the play lasts two and a half hours, including the interval

si prega di spegnere i telefoni cellulari
please turn off your mobile phones

PARTIES AND CLUBS

Expressing yourself

I'm having a little leaving party tonight
do una piccola festa d'addio stasera
do oona peekola festa daddee-o stasayra

should I bring something to drink?
porto qualcosa da bere?
porto kwalkoza da bayray?

we could go to a club afterwards
potremmo andare in discoteca dopo
potraymo andaray een deeskotayca dopo

will you let me back in when I come back?
mi lascia rientrare quando ritorno?
mee lasha ree-entraray kwando reetorno?

thanks, but I'm with my boyfriend
grazie, ma sono con il mio ragazzo
gratsee-ay, ma sono kon eel mee-o ragatso

do you have to pay to get in?
l'ingresso è a pagamento?
leengresso ay a pagamento?

I have to meet someone inside
devo vedere qualcuno dentro
dayvo vaydayray kwalkoono dentro

the DJ's really cool
il DJ è da sballo
eel deejay ay da zballo

do you come here often?
vieni qui spesso?
vee-aynee kwee spesso?

can I buy you a drink?
posso offrirti da bere?
posso ofreertee da bayray?

no thanks, I don't smoke
no grazie, non fumo
no gratsee-ay, non foomo

Understanding

consumazione gratuita	free drink
guardaroba	cloakroom
15 euro dopo mezzanotte	15 euros after midnight

c'è una festa a casa di Brunella
there's a party at Brunella's place

vuoi ballare?
do you want to dance?

hai da accendere?
have you got a light?

hai una sigaretta?
have you got a cigarette?

ci possiamo rivedere?
can we see each other again?

ti posso accompagnare a casa?
can I see you home?

TOURISM AND SIGHTSEEING

Most towns have a tourist information centre (**ufficio turistico**), run by the Italian State Tourist Board or **ENIT** (**Ente Nazionale Italiano per il Turismo**) where you can get maps and find out about local places of interest, including museums and art galleries, as well as information on local festivals and special events. They also provide information on transport and help with finding accommodation. It's always possible to get some of this information in English before your trip by contacting the Italian Tourist Office in London.

The basics

ancient	antico *anteeko*
area	area *aray-a*
castle	castello *kastello*
cathedral	cattedrale *kataydralay*
century	secolo *saykolo*
church	chiesa *kee-ayza*
exhibition	mostra *mostra*
gallery	galleria *gallayree-a*
modern art	arte moderna *artay moderna*
mosque	moschea *moskay-a*
museum	museo *moozay-o*
painting	dipinto *deepeento*
park	parco *parko*
ruins	rovine *roveenay*
sculpture	scultura *skooltoora*
statue	statua *statoo-a*
street map	pianta *pee-anta*
synagogue	sinagoga *seenagoga*
tour guide	guida turistica *gweeda tooreesteeka*
tourist	turista *tooreesta*

| **tourist information centre** | ufficio turistico *oofeecho tooreesteeko* |
| **town centre** | centro *chentro* |

Expressing yourself

I'd like some information on …
vorrei delle informazioni su …
voray-ee dellay eenformatsee-onee soo …

can you tell me where the tourist office is?
mi può dire dov'è l'ufficio turistico?
mee poo-o deeray dovay loofeecho tooreesteeko?

do you have a street map of the town?
ha una pianta della città?
a oona pee-anta della cheeta?

I was told there's an old abbey you can visit
mi hanno detto che c'è una vecchia abbazia che si può visitare
mee anno detto kay chay oona vekee-a abatsee-a kay see poo-o veezeetaray

can you show me where it is on the map?
mi può far vedere dov'è sulla cartina?
mee poo-o far vaydayray dovay soola karteena?

how do you get there?
come ci si va?
komay chee see va?

is it free?
è gratuito?
ay gratoo-eeto?

when was it built?
quando è stato costruito?
kwando ay stato kostroo-eeto?

Understanding

aperto	open
centro storico	old town
chiuso	closed
ingresso gratuito	admission free
gotico	Gothic
guerra	war
invasione	invasion

TOURISM, SIGHTSEEING

lavori di restauro	restoration work
medievale	mediaeval
ristrutturazione	renovation
romanico	Romanesque
siete qui	you are here *(on a map)*
visita guidata	guided tour

deve chiedere sul posto
you'll have to ask when you get there

la prossima visita guidata è alle due
the next guided tour starts at 2 o'clock

MUSEUMS, EXHIBITIONS AND MONUMENTS

Expressing yourself

I've heard there's a very good ... exhibition on at the moment
ho sentito che attualmente c'è una mostra di ... molto bella
o senteeto kay atoo-almentay chay oona mostra dee ... molto bella

how much is it to get in?
quanto costa il biglietto?
kwanto kosta eel beelyetto?

is it open on Sundays?
è aperto di domenica?
ay aperto dee domayneeka?

is this ticket valid for the exhibition as well?
il biglietto vale anche per la mostra?
eel beelyetto valay ankay per la mostra?

are there any discounts for young people?
ci sono sconti per i giovani?
chee sono skontee per ee jovannee?

two concessions and one full price, please
due biglietti ridotti e uno intero, per favore
doo-ay beelyettee reedotee ay oono eentayro, per favoray

I have a student card
ho la tessera studentesca
o la tessayra stoodenteska

Understanding

audioguida	audioguide
biglietteria	ticket office
mostra permanente	permanent exhibition
mostra temporanea	temporary exhibition
senso della visita	this way
si prega di non toccare	please do not touch
vietato fotografare	no photography
vietato usare il flash	no flash photography

il biglietto di ingresso per il museo costa …
admission to the museum costs …

con questo biglietto si può accedere anche alla mostra
this ticket also allows you access to the exhibition

ha la tessera studentesca?
do you have your student card?

GIVING YOUR IMPRESSIONS

Expressing yourself

it's beautiful
è bello
ay bello

it was beautiful
è stato bello
ay stato bello

it's fantastic
è fantastico
ay fantasteeko

it was fantastic
è stato fantastico
ay stato fantasteeko

I really enjoyed it
mi è piaciuto molto
mee ay pee-achooto molto

I didn't like it that much
non mi è piaciuto un granché
non mee ay pee-achooto oon grankay

it was a bit boring
è stato un po' noioso
ay stato oon po noyozo

it's expensive for what it is
è caro per quello che è
ay karo per kwello kay ay

I'm not really a fan of modern art
non sono un patito di arte moderna
non sono oon patteeto dee artay moderna

it's very touristy
è molto turistico
ay molto tooreesteeko

it was really crowded
c'era tantissima gente
chayra tanteesseema gentay

we didn't go in the end, the queue was too long
alla fine non ci siamo andati, c'era troppa coda
alla feenay non chee see-amo andatee, chayra troppa koda

we didn't have time to see everything
non abbiamo avuto il tempo di vedere tutto
non abbee-amo avooto eel tempo dee vaydayray tooto

Understanding

famoso	famous
pittoresco	picturesque
tipico	typical
tradizionale	traditional

dovete proprio andare a vedere …
you really must go and see …

vi consiglio di andare …
I recommend going to …

c'è una vista magnifica su tutta la città
there's a wonderful view over the whole city

è diventato un po' troppo turistico
it's become a bit too touristy

la costa è stata completamente deturpata
the coast has been completely ruined

SPORTS AND GAMES

Italians love football: every town has a team, and big cities often have two. The most famous are Rome's **AS Roma** and **Lazio**, Milan's **Milan A.C.** and **Inter**, and Turin's **Torino** and **Juventus**.

Some of the world's best skiing can be found in the Italian Alps. The Dolomites region and the Milky Way (**la Via Lattea**) each have hundreds of kilometres of slopes.

Cycling is also popular, and the most famous event is the **Giro d'Italia** or the Tour of Italy.

The basics

ball	palla *pala*
basketball	pallacanestro *palakannestro*
bicycle	bicicletta *beecheekletta*
board game	gioco da tavolo *joko da tavolo*
cards	carte *kartay*
chess	scacchi *skakkee*
cross-country skiing	sci di fondo *shee dee fondo*
cycling	ciclismo *cheekleezmo*
downhill skiing	sci alpino *shee alpeeno*
football	calcio *kalcho*
hiking path	sentiero *sentee-ayro*
match	partita *parteeta*
mountain biking	mountain bike *mowntem ba-eek*
pool	pool *pool (game)*
rugby	rugby *ragbee*
ski	sci *shee*
snowboarding	snowboard *znobord*
sport	sport *sport*
surfing	surf *serf*
swimming	nuoto *noo-oto*

swimming pool	piscina *peesheena*
table football	calcetto *kalchetto*
tennis	tennis *tennees*
trip	gita *jeeta*
to go hiking	fare delle escursioni *faray dellay eskoorsee-onee*
to have a game of ...	fare una partita a ... *faray oona parteeta a ...*
to play	giocare *jokaray*

Expressing yourself

I'd like to hire ... for an hour
vorrei noleggiare ... per un'ora
voray-ee nolejaray ... per oonora

are there ... lessons available?
è possibile prendere lezioni di ...?
ay posseebeelay prendayray letsee-onee dee ...?

how much is it per person per hour?
quanto costa a testa all'ora?
kwanto kosta a testa allora?

I'm not very sporty
non sono molto sportivo
non sono molto sporteevo

I've never done it before
non l'ho mai fatto prima d'ora
non lo ma-ee fatto preema dora

I've done it once or twice, a long time ago
l'ho fatto una o due volte, molto tempo fa
lo fatto oona o doo-ay voltay, molto tempo fa

I'm exhausted!
sono distrutto!
sono deestrooto!

we played ...
abbiamo giocato a ...
abbee-amo jokato a ...

I'd like to go and watch a football match
mi piacerebbe andare a vedere una partita di calcio
mee pee-achayrebbay andaray a vaydayray oona parteeta dee kalcho

shall we stop for a picnic?
ci fermiamo per fare un picnic?
chee fermee-amo per faray oon peekneek?

SPORTS AND GAMES

Understanding

noleggio di ... ... for hire

ha qualche nozione o è un principiante assoluto?
do you have any experience, or are you a complete beginner?

c'è una cauzione di ...
there is a deposit of ...

l'assicurazione è obbligatoria e costa ...
insurance is compulsory and costs ...

HIKING

Expressing yourself

are there any hiking paths around here?
ci sono dei sentieri da queste parti?
chee sono day-ee sentee-ayree da kwestay partee?

can you recommend any good walks in the area?
può consigliarci qualche escursione a piedi interessante in zona?
poo-o konseelyarchee kwalkay eskoorsee-onay a pee-aydee eentayressantay een dzona?

I've heard there's a nice walk by the lake
ho sentito che c'è una bella passeggiata in riva al lago
o senteeto kay chay oona bella passejata een reeva al lago

we're looking for a short walk somewhere round here
cerchiamo una breve escursione a piedi da fare in zona
cherkee-amo oona brayvay eskoorsee-onay a pee-aydee da faray een dzona

can I hire hiking boots?
posso noleggiare degli scarponi da montagna?
posso nolejaray delyee skarponee da montanya?

is it very steep?
è molto ripido?
ay molto reepeedo?

how long does the hike take?
quanto dura l'escursione?
kwanto doora leskoorsee-onay?

is the path waymarked?
il sentiero è segnato?
eel sentee-ayro ay senyato?

where's the start of the path?
dove comincia il sentiero?
dovay komeencha eel sentee-ayro?

is it a circular path?
è un sentiero circolare?
ay oon sentee-ayro cheerkolaray?

Understanding

durata media   average duration *(of walk)*

è un'escursione di circa tre ore, comprese le soste
it's about 3 hours' walk including rest stops

portatevi una giacca impermeabile e delle scarpe da montagna
bring a waterproof jacket and some walking shoes

SKIING AND SNOWBOARDING

Expressing yourself

I'd like to hire skis, poles and boots
vorrei noleggiare sci, racchette e scarponi
voray-ee nolejaray shee, rakkettay ay skarponee

I'd like to hire a snowboard
vorrei noleggiare uno snowboard
voray-ee nolejaray oono znobord

they're too big/small
sono troppo grandi/piccoli
sono tropo grandee/peekolee

a day pass
un giornaliero
oon jornalee-ayro

I'm a complete beginner
sono un principiante assoluto
sono oon preencheepee-antay assolooto

Understanding

ovovia	cable car
seggiovia	chair lift
skilift	ski lift
ski-pass	lift pass

OTHER SPORTS

Expressing yourself

where can we hire bikes?
dove possiamo noleggiare delle bici?
dovay possee-amo nolejaray dellay beechee?

are there any cycle paths?
ci sono delle piste ciclabili?
chee sono dellay peestay cheeklabbeelee?

does anyone have a football?
qualcuno ha un pallone?
kwalkoono a oon palonay?

which team do you support?
per che squadra tieni?
per kay skwadra tee-aynee?

I support ...
tengo per ...
tengo per ...

I've never been diving before
non ho mai fatto immersioni
non o ma-ee fatto emmersee-onee

is there an open-air swimming pool?
c'è una piscina all'aperto?
chay oona peesheena allaperto?

I'd like to take beginners' sailing lessons
vorrei prendere delle lezioni di vela per principianti
voray-ee prendayray dellay letsee-onee dee vayla per preencheepee-antee

I run for half an hour every morning
faccio mezzora di footing tutte le mattine
facho metsora dee footeeng tootay lay matteenay

what do I do if the kayak capsizes?
cosa faccio se il kayak si ribalta?
koza facho say eel ka-yak see reebalta?

Understanding

c'è un campo da tennis comunale non lontano dalla stazione
there's a public tennis court not far from the station

il campo da tennis è occupato
the tennis court's occupied

è la prima volta che monta a cavallo?
is this the first time you've been horse-riding?

sa nuotare?
can you swim?

giochi a pallacanestro?
do you play basketball?

INDOOR GAMES

Expressing yourself

shall we have a game of cards?
facciamo una partita a carte?
fachamo oona parteeta a kartay?

does anyone know any good card games?
qualcuno conosce un gioco di carte divertente?
kwalkoono konoshay oon joko dee kartay deevertentay?

is anyone up for a game of Monopoly®?
qualcuno ha voglia di fare una partita a Monopoli®?
kwalkoono a volya dee faray oona parteeta a Monopoli?

it's your turn
tocca a te
toka a tay

Understanding

hai un mazzo di carte?
do you have a pack of cards?

sai giocare a scacchi?
do you know how to play chess?

Some informal expressions

sono a pezzi I'm knackered
mi ha schiacciato he wiped the floor with me

SHOPPING

Shops are generally open from 9am to 7.30pm and are closed on Monday mornings, except for camera shops (**fotografi**) and opticians (**ottici**), which are closed all day on Monday, and grocery shops (**negozi di alimentari**) and bakeries (**panetterie**) which are closed on Wednesday afternoons.

Note that small shops usually close between 1 and 4pm.

More upmarket shops tend to be found in city centres, while big shopping centres and hypermarkets are generally found on the outskirts.

Markets are an important feature of Italian life. Some outdoor markets take place every morning and all day on Saturdays, with stalls selling not just food, but also clothes, shoes, etc. Other outdoor markets, generally not dedicated to food, take place once or twice a week. You can find very high-quality goods at competitive prices in some markets. Note that bargaining is only possible in markets. Many Italians prefer to buy their fruit and vegetables from markets, as well as fish, meat, cheese, and local specialities. You can of course buy food in the many supermarkets and hypermarkets, as well as in small local shops, although these are disappearing in big cities

Cigarettes are sold in traditional tobacconists as well as from machines.

Note that Italian dress sizes vary slightly from the rest of Europe: a European 38 (UK 10) is an Italian 42, a European 40 (UK 12) is an Italian 44 and so on (see Conversion Tables p. 190).

The basics

bakery	panetteria *pannetteree-a*
butcher's	macelleria *machelleree-a*
cash desk	cassa *kassa*
cheap	economico *aykonomeeko*
checkout	cassa *kassa*
clothes	abbigliamento *abbeelyamento*

department store	grande magazzino *granday magadzeeno*
expensive	caro *karo*
gram	grammo *grammo*
greengrocer's	fruttivendolo *frooteevendolo*
hypermarket	ipermercato *eepermerkato*
kilo	chilo *keelo*
present	regalo *raygalo*
price	prezzo *pretso*
receipt	scontrino *skontreeno*
sales assistant	commesso *commesso*
sales	saldi *saldee*
shop	negozio *naygotsee-o*
shopping centre	centro commerciale *chentro commerchalay*
souvenir	souvenir *soovayneer*
supermarket	supermercato *soopermerkato*
to buy	comprare *kompraray*
to cost	costare *kostaray*
to pay	pagare *pagaray*
to refund	rimborsare *reemborsaray*
to sell	vendere *vendayray*

Expressing yourself

is there a supermarket near here?
c'è un supermercato da queste parti?
chay oon soopermerkato da kwestay partee?

where can I buy cigarettes?
dove posso comprare delle sigarette?
dovay posso kompraray dellay seegarrettay?

I'd like …
vorrei …
voray-ee …

I'm looking for …
sto cercando …
sto cherkando …

do you sell ...?
vendete ...?
vendaytay ...?

can you order it for me?
può ordinarmelo?
poo-o ordeenarmaylo?

do you know where I might find ...?
sa dove potrei trovare ...?
sa dovay potray-ee trovaray ...?

how much is this?
quanto costa questo?
kwanto kosta kwesto?

I'll take it
lo prendo
lo prendo

I haven't got much money
non ho molti soldi
non o moltee soldee

I haven't got enough money
non ho abbastanza soldi
non o abastantsa soldee

that's everything, thanks
basta così, grazie
basta kozee, gratsee-ay

can I have a (plastic) bag?
posso avere un sacchetto (di plastica)?
posso avayray oon sakketto (dee plasteeka)?

I think you've made a mistake with my change
penso che si sia sbagliato dandomi il resto
penso kay see see-a zbalyato dandomee eel resto

Understanding

aperto da ... a ...   open from ... to ...

chiuso la domenica/
dalle 13.00 alle 15.00
closed Sundays/1pm to 3pm

offerta speciale
special offer

saldi
sales

desidera altro?
will there be anything else?

vuole un sacchetto?
would you like a bag?

PAYING

SHOPPING

Expressing yourself

where do I pay?
dove si paga?
dovay see paga?

how much do I owe you?
quanto le devo?
kwanto lay dayvo?

could you write it down for me, please?
può scrivermelo, per favore?
poo-o skreevermaylo, per favoray?

can I pay by credit card?
posso pagare con la carta di credito?
posso pagaray kon la karta dee craydeeto?

I'll pay in cash
pago in contanti
pago een kontantee

can I have a receipt?
posso avere una ricevuta?
posso avayray oona reecheevoota?

I'm sorry, I haven't got any change
mi dispiace, non ho spiccioli
mee deespee-achay, non o speecholee

Understanding

paghi alla cassa
pay at the cash desk

come desidera pagare?
how would you like to pay?

non ha spiccioli?
don't you have any change?

può firmare qui, per favore?
could you sign here, please?

ha un documento di indentità?
have you got any ID?

FOOD

> **Making sense of abbreviations**
>
> **hg** (= **ettogrammo** or **etto**)   hectogram (= 100 grams)
>
> Note that when buying cold meats, you should specify the amount in **etti** rather than asking for a certain number of slices.

Expressing yourself

where can I buy food around here?
dove posso comprare da mangiare da queste parti?
dovay posso kompraray da manjaray da kwestay partee?

is there a bakery around here?
c'è una panetteria nei dintorni?
chay oona pannetteree-a nay-ee deentornee?

I'm looking for the cereal aisle
sto cercando il reparto dei cereali
sto cherkando eel rayparto day-ee chayree-alee

I'd like a hundred grams of ham
vorrei un etto di prosciutto
voray-ee oon etto dee proshooto

I'd like some of that goat's cheese
vorrei un pezzo di quel formaggio di capra
voray-ee oon petso dee kwel formajo dee capra

is there a market?
c'è un mercato?
chay oon merkato?

it's for four people
è per quattro persone
ay per kwatro personay

about 300 grams
circa tre etti
cheerka tray ettee

a kilo of apples, please
un chilo di mele, per favore
oon keelo dee maylay, per favoray

a bit less/more
un po' di meno/di più
oon po dee mayno/dee pyoo

can I taste it?
lo posso assaggiare?
lo posso assajaray?

does it travel well?
si conserva bene in viaggio?
see konserva baynay een veeajo?

Understanding

biologico	organic
da consumarsi entro il ...	best before ...
fatto in casa	homemade
gastronomia	delicatessen
specialità regionali	local specialities

c'è mercato tutti i giorni fino all'una
there's a market every day until 1pm

c'è un negozio di alimentari qui all'angolo che è aperto fino a tardi
there's a grocer's just on the corner that's open late

CLOTHES

Expressing yourself

I'm looking for the menswear department
sto cercando il reparto uomo
sto cherkando eel rayparto oo-omo

no thanks, I'm just looking
no, grazie, do solo un'occhiata
no, gratsee-ay, do solo oonokee-ata

can I try it on?
lo posso provare?
lo posso provaray?

I take a size 39 *(in shoes)*
porto il trentanove
porto eel trentanovay

it doesn't fit	**it's too big/small**
non va bene	è troppo grande/piccolo
non va baynay	*ay tropo granday/peekolo*

I'd like to try the one in the window
vorrei provare quello in vetrina
voray-ee provaray kwello een vaytreena

where are the changing rooms?
dove sono le cabine di prova?
dovay sono lay kabbeenay dee prova?

do you have it in another colour?
ce l'avete in un altro colore?
chay lavaytay een oon altro koloray?

do you have it in a smaller/bigger size?
ce l'avete in una taglia più piccola/più grande?
chay lavaytay een oona talya pyoo peekola/pyoo granday?

do you have them in red?	**yes, that's fine; I'll take them**
ce li avete rossi?	sì, va bene, li prendo
chay lee avaytay rossee?	*see, va baynay, lee prendo*
no, I don't like it	**I'll think about it**
no, non mi piace	ci devo pensare
no, non mee pee-achay	*chee dayvo pensaray*

I'd like to return this: it doesn't fit
vorrei dare indietro questo, non va bene
voray-ee daray eendee-aytro kwesto, non va baynay

this ... has a hole in it: can I get a refund?
questo ... ha un buco: posso farmi rimborsare?
kwesto ... a oon booko: posso farmee reemborsaray?

Understanding

abbigliamento da donna	ladieswear
abbigliamento da uomo	menswear
abbligliamento infantile	children's clothes
aperto la domenica	open Sunday
biancheria intima	lingerie

cabine di prova
changing rooms

gli articoli in saldo non possono essere cambiati
sale items cannot be returned

buongiorno, desidera?
hello, can I help you?

lo abbiamo solo in blu o nero
we only have it in blue or black

le sta bene
it suits you

le va bene
it's a good fit

non ne abbiamo più in questa taglia
we don't have any left in that size

lo può riportare se non va bene
you can bring it back if it doesn't fit

SOUVENIRS AND PRESENTS

Expressing yourself

I'm looking for a present to take home
sto cercando un regalo da portare a casa
sto cherkando oon raygalo da portaray a kaza

I'd like something that's easy to transport
vorrei qualcosa che sia facile da trasportare
voray-ee kwalkoza kay see-a facheelay da trasportaray

it's for a little girl of four
è per una bambina di quattro anni
ay per oona bambeena dee kwatro annee

could you gift-wrap it for me?
mi può fare un pacco regalo?
mee poo-o faray oon pakko raygalo?

Understanding

di legno/d'argento/ d'oro/di lana
made of wood/of silver/of gold/of wool

fatto a mano
handmade

prodotto artigianale
traditionally made product

quanto vuole spendere?
how much do you want to spend?

è per un regalo?
is it for a present?

è tipico della regione
it's typical of the region

Some informal expressions

costa un occhio della testa it costs an arm and a leg
è un furto it's a rip-off
è regalato it's a steal

The basics

black and white	bianco e nero *bee-anko ay nayro*
camera	macchina fotografica *makeena fotografeeka*
colour	a colori *a koloree*
copy	copia *kopee-a*
digital camera	macchina fotografica digitale *makeena fotografeeka deejeetalay*
disposable camera	macchina fotografica usa e getta *makeena fotografeeka ooza ay jetta*
exposure	esposizione *espozeetsee-onay*
film	rullino *rooleeno*
flash	flash *flesh*
glossy	su carta lucida *soo karta loocheeda*
matt	su carta opaca *soo karta opaka*
memory card	scheda di memoria *skayda dee maymoree-a*
negative	negativo *naygatteevo*
passport photo	foto tessera *foto tessayra*
photo booth	cabina automatica per foto tessera *kabbeena owtomatteeka per foto tessayra*
reprint	ristampa *reestampa*
slide	diapositiva *dee-apozeeteeva*
to get photos developed	far sviluppare delle foto *far zveelooparay dellay foto*
to take a photo/ photos	fare una foto/delle foto *faray oona foto/dellay foto*

Expressing yourself

could you take a photo of us, please?
ci potrebbe fare una foto, per favore?
chee potrebbay faray oona foto, per favoray?

you just have to press this button
basta premere questo pulsante
basta praymeray kwesto poolsantay

PHOTOS

85

I'd like a 200 ASA colour film
vorrei un rullino a colori duecento ASA
voray-ee oon rooleeno a koloree doo-aychento aza

do you have black and white films?
avete dei rullini in bianco e nero?
avaytay day-ee rooleenee een bee-anko ay nayro?

how much is it to develop a film of 36 photos?
quanto costa lo sviluppo di un rullino da trentasei pose?
kwanto kosta lo zveeloopo dee oon rooleeno da trentasay-ee posay?

I'd like to have this film developed
vorrei far sviluppare questo rullino
voray-ee far zveelooparay kwesto rooleeno

I'd like extra copies of some of the photos
vorrei delle copie di alcune foto
voray-ee dellay kopee-ay dee alkoonay foto

three copies of this one and two of this one
tre copie di questa e due di questa
tray kopee-ay dee kwesta ay doo-ay dee kwesta

can I print my digital photos here?
posso far stampare delle foto digitali qui?
posso far stamparay dellay foto deejeetallee kwee?

can you put these photos on a CD for me?
mi può copiare queste foto su un CD?
mee poo-o kopee-aray kwestay foto soo oon cheedee?

I don't know what it is
non so cosa sia
non so koza see-a

do you sell memory cards?
vendete schede di memoria?
vendaytay skayday dee memoree-a?

I've come to pick up my photos
sono venuto a ritirare le mie foto
sono vaynooto a reeteeraray le mee-ay foto

I've got a problem with my camera
ho un problema con la mia macchina fotografica
o oon problayma kon la mee-a makeena fotografeeka

the flash doesn't work
il flash non funziona
eel flesh non foontsee-ona

Understanding

formato standard	standard format
foto su CD	photos on CD
servizio espresso	express service
sviluppo in un'ora	photos developed in one hour

forse la batteria è scarica
maybe the battery's dead

abbiamo una macchina per stampare le foto digitali
we have a machine for printing digital photos

per quando le vuole?	**a quale nome, per favore?**
when do you want them for?	what's the name, please?

le possiamo sviluppare in un'ora
we can develop them in an hour

le sue foto saranno pronte per giovedì a mezzogiorno
your photos will be ready on Thursday at noon

Banks are generally open from 8:30am to 1:30pm and most are also open for a shorter time in the afternoon, Monday to Friday. Cashpoints display a **bancomat** logo. Credit cards are accepted in most shops and restaurants.

The basics

bank	banca *banka*
bank account	conto (bancario) *konto (bankaree-o)*
banknote	banconota *bankonota*
bureau de change	ufficio cambio *oofeecho kambee-o*
cashpoint	bancomat *bankomat*
cheque	assegno *assenyo*
coin	moneta *monayta*
commission	commissione *komeessee-onay*
credit card	carta di credito *karta dee craydeeto*
PIN (number)	codice segreto *kodeechay saygrayto*
transfer	bonifico *boneefeeko*
traveller's cheque	traveller's cheque *traveler chek*
withdrawal	prelievo *praylee-ayvo*
to change	cambiare *kambee-aray*
to withdraw	prelevare *praylayvaray*

Expressing yourself

where I can get some money changed?
dove posso cambiare dei soldi?
dovay posso kambee-aray day-ee soledee?

where is the nearest bank?
dov'è la banca più vicina?
dovay la banka pyoo veecheena?

I'm looking for a cashpoint
sto cercando un bancomat®
sto cherkando oon bankomat

I'd like to change £100
vorrei cambiare cento sterline
voray-ee kambee-aray chento sterleenay

what commission do you charge?
quant'è la commissione?
kwantay la komeessee-onay?

I'd like to transfer some money
vorrei fare un bonifico
voray-ee faray oon boneefeeko

I'd like to report the loss of my credit card
vorrei denunciare la perdita della carta di credito
voray-ee daynooncharay la perdeeta della karta dee craydeeto

the cashpoint has swallowed my card
il bancomat mi ha mangiato la carta
eel bankomat mee a manjato la karta

Understanding

inserire la carta
please insert your card

fuori servizio
out of service

prelievo con ricevuta
withdrawal with receipt

digitare il codice
please enter your PIN number

scegliere l'importo
please select the amount you require

prelievo senza ricevuta
withdrawal without receipt

POST OFFICES

(i)

Most offices are open from 8.30am to 1.30pm, Monday to Friday, and close earlier on Saturdays, though in small villages the post office may be open only some days and for only a few hours. In towns and cities, the main post office stays open until 5pm.

You can buy stamps in tobacconists as well as in post offices.

The basics

airmail	via aerea *vee-a a-ayree-a*
envelope	busta *boosta*
letter	lettera *lettayra*
mail	posta *posta*
parcel	pacco *pakko*
post	posta *posta*
postbox	buca delle lettere *booka dellay lettayray*
postcard	cartolina *kartoleena*
postcode	codice postale *kodeechay postalay*
post office	ufficio postale *oofeecho postalay*
stamp	francobollo *frankobolo*
to post	imbucare *eembookaray*
to send	spedire *spaydeeray*
to write	scrivere *screeveray*

Expressing yourself

is there a post office around here?
c'è un ufficio postale qui vicino?
chay oon oofeecho postalay kwee veecheeno?

is there a postbox near here?
c'è una buca delle lettere qui vicino?
chay oona booka dellay lettayray kwee veecheeno?

is the post office open on Saturdays?
l'ufficio postale è aperto di sabato?
loofeecho postalay ay apperto dee sabato?

what time does the post office close?
a che ora chiude l'ufficio postale?
a kay ora kee-ooday loofeecho postalay?

is there any post for me?
c'è posta per me?
chay posta per may?

do you sell stamps?
vendete francobolli?
vendaytay frankobolee?

I'd like … stamps for the UK, please
vorrei … francobolli per il Regno Unito, per favore
voray-ee … frankobolee per eel raynyo ooneeto, per favoray

how long will it take to arrive?
quanto ci metterà ad arrivare?
kwanto chee mettera ad arreevaray?

where can I buy envelopes?
dove posso comprare delle buste?
dovay posso kompraray dellay boostay?

Understanding

fragile	fragile
mittente	sender
prima levata	first collection
ultima levata	last collection

ci vorranno tra i tre e i cinque giorni
it'll take between three and five days

INTERNET CAFÉS AND E-MAIL

The basics

at sign	chiocciola *kee-ochola*
e-mail address	indirizzo e-mail *eendeereetso ee-mayl*
e-mail	e-mail *ee-mayl*
Internet café	Internet café *eenternet kafay*
key	tasto *tasto*
keyboard	tastiera *tastee-ayra*
to copy	copiare *kopee-aray*
to cut	tagliare *talyee-aray*
to delete	cancellare *kancellaray*
to download	scaricare *skarreekaray*
to e-mail somebody	mandare un'e-mail a qualcuno *mandaray oonee-mayl a kwalkoono*
to paste	incollare *eenkolaray*
to receive	ricevere *reechayvayray*
to save	salvare *salvaray*
to send an e-mail	mandare un'e-mail *mandaray oonee-mayl*

Expressing yourself

is there an Internet café near here?
c'è un Internet café da queste parti?
chay oon eenternet kafay da kwestay partee?

how do I get online?
come ci si connette?
komay chee see konnettay?

do you have an e-mail address?
ha un indirizzo e-mail?
a oon eendeereetso ee-mayl?

I'd just like to check my e-mails
vorrei solo controllare le mie e-mail
voray-ee solo kontrolaray lay mee-ay ee-mayl

would you mind helping me? I'm not sure what to do
le dispiacerebbe aiutarmi? non so bene come fare
lay deespee-achayrebbay ayootarmee? non so baynay comay faray

I can't find the at-sign on this keyboard
non trovo la chiocciola su questa tastiera
non trovo la kee-ochola soo kwesta tastee-ayra

there's something wrong with the computer: it's frozen
c'è qualcosa che non va con il computer: si è bloccato
chay kwalkoza kay non va kon eel compyooter: see ay blokato

how much will it be for half an hour?
quanto costa una mezzora?
kwanto kosta oona medzora?

it's not working
non funziona
non foontseeona

when do I pay?
quando si paga?
kwando see paga?

Understanding

posta in arrivo   inbox
posta inviata   outbox

deve aspettare una ventina di minuti
you'll have to wait for 20 minutes or so

chieda pure se non sa come fare
just ask if you're not sure what to do

inserire la password per connettersi
just enter this password to log on

TELEPHONE

All public telephones take phonecards, while some take coins as well. You can buy phonecards in tobacconists. Now that mobile phones have become so widespread, public telephones are disappearing and those that can still be found are often out of order.

When giving telephone numbers, Italians read out the digits one by one. For example, 02 4372388 is said as zero, due, quattro, tre, sette, due, tre, otto, otto.

To call the UK from Italy, dial 00 44 followed by the full phone number, minus the first 0 of the area code. To call Italy from the UK, dial 00 39 followed by the area code, including the first 0 of the area code. When you are in Italy, you always need to dial the area code, even when you're making a local phone call. The number for directory enquiries in Italy is 412 (**quattrocentrododici**).

The basics

answering machine	segreteria telefonica *saygraytayree-a taylayfoneeka*
call	chiamata *kee-amata*
directory enquiries	ricerca elenco abbonati *reecherka aylenko abbonattee*
hello	pronto? *pronto?*
international call	chiamata internazionale *kee-amata eenternatsee-onalay*
local call	chiamata urbana *kee-amata oorbana*
message	messaggio *messajo*
mobile	cellulare *cheloolaray*
national call	chiamata nazionale *kee-amata natsee-onalay*
phone book	elenco telefonico *aylenko taylayfoneeko*
phone box	cabina telefonica *kabbeena taylayfoneeka*
phone call	telefonata *taylayfonata*

phone number	numero telefonico *numayro taylayfoneeko*
phonecard	scheda telefonica *skayda taylayfoneeka*
ringtone	suoneria *soo-oneree-a*
telephone	telefono *taylayfono*
top-up card	ricarica
Yellow Pages®	Pagine Gialle® *pajeenay jallay*
to call somebody	chiamare qualcuno *kee-amaray kwalkoono*
to phone	telefonare *taylayfonaray*

Expressing yourself

where can I buy a phonecard?
dove posso comprare una scheda telefonica?
dovay posso kompraray oona skayda taylayfoneeka?

a ...-euro phonecard, please
una scheda telefonica da ... euro, per favore
oona skayda taylayfoneeka da ... ayooro, per favoray

I'd like to make a reverse-charge call
vorrei fare una chiamata a carico del destinatario
voray-ee faray oona kee-amata a karreeko del desteenatarree-o

is there a phone box near here, please?
c'è una cabina telefonica qui vicino?
chay oona kabbeena taylayfoneeka kwee veeecheeno?

can I plug my phone in here to recharge it?
posso mettere il mio cellulare in carica qui?
posso mettayray eel mee-o cheloolaray een karreeka kwee?

where can I contact you?
dove la posso trovare?
dovay la posso trovaray?

do you have a mobile number?
ha un numero di cellulare?
a oon noomayro dee cheloolaray?

did you get my message?
ha ricevuto il mio messaggio?
a reechayvooto eel mee-o messajo?

Understanding

il numero richiesto non è attribuito
the number you have dialled has not been recognized

premere il tasto cancelletto
please press the hash key

MAKING A CALL

Expressing yourself

hello, this is David Brown (speaking)
pronto? sono David Brown
pronto? sono David Brown

hello, could I speak to..., please?
pronto? potrei parlare con ..., per favore?
pronto? potray-ee parlaray kon ..., per favoray?

hello, is that Luigi?
pronto? sei Luigi?
pronto? say-ee loo-eejee?

do you speak English?
parla inglese?
parla eenglayzay?

could you speak more slowly, please?
può parlare più lentamente, per favore?
poo-o parlaray pyoo lentamentay, per favoray?

I can't hear you, could you speak up, please?
non la sento, può parlare più forte, per favore?
non la sento, poo-o parlaray pyoo fortay, per favoray?

could you tell him/her I called?
può dirgli/dirle che ho chiamato?
poo-o deerlyee/deerlay kay o kee-amato?

could you ask him/her to call me back?
può chiedergli/chiederle di richiamarmi?
poo-o kee-ayderlyee/kee-ayderlay dee reekee-amarmee?

I'll call back later
richiamo più tardi
reekee-amo pyoo tardee

thank you, goodbye
grazie, arrivederci
gratsee-ay, arreevayderchee

my name is … and my number is …
mi chiamo … e il mio numero è …
mee kee-amo … ay eel mee-o noomayro ay …

do you know when he/she might be available?
sa quando lo/la posso trovare?
sa kwando lo/la posso trovaray?

Understanding

chi parla?
who's calling?

ha sbagliato numero
you've got the wrong number

gli/le dico che ha chiamato
I'll tell him/her you called

gli/le dico di richiamarla
I'll ask him/her to call you back

attenda in linea
hold on

glielo/gliela passo
I'll just hand you over to him/her

vuole lasciare un messaggio?
do you want to leave a message?

in questo momento non c'è
he's/she's not here at the moment

PROBLEMS

Expressing yourself

I don't know the code
non conosco il prefisso
non konosko eel prayfeesso

it's engaged
è occupato
ay okoopato

there's no reply
non risponde nessuno
non reesponday nessoono

I can't get a signal
non c'è segnale
non chay saynyalay

I tried to call him, but I couldn't get through
ho provato a chiamarlo, ma non sono riuscito a parlargli
o provato a kee-amarlo, ma non sono ree-oosheeto a parlarlyee

I don't have much credit left on my phone
ho poco credito sul cellulare
o poko craydeeto sool cheloolaray

we're about to get cut off
sta per cadere la linea
sta per kadayray la leenay-a

the reception's really bad
si sente malissimo
see sentay malleesseemo

Understanding

ti sento a malapena
I can hardly hear you

la linea è disturbata
it's a bad line

Common abbreviations

uff. = ufficio work (number)
cell. = cellulare mobile (number)

Some informal expressions

telefonino mobile
dare un colpo di telefono a qualcuno to give somebody a ring
sbattere il telefono in faccia a qualcuno
to slam the phone down on somebody

If you are an EU national, apply for the European Health Insurance Card at your local post office before you travel to Italy. This will entitle you to free or reduced-cost medical care during your visit. Only state-provided emergency treatment is covered, which you will receive on the same terms as Italian nationals.

You can get a list of GPs from the local health authority offices or **ASL** (**Azienda Sanitaria Locale**).

Chemists (**farmacie**) have the same opening hours as most shops and they usually close for lunch. If you need their services outside normal working hours, you can find a list of local duty chemists displayed in the window.

In a medical emergency, dial **118** for first aid (**pronto soccorso**). The emergency medical service is called **la guardia medica**.

The basics

allergy	allergia *allerjee-a*
ambulance	ambulanza *amboolantsa*
aspirin	aspirina *aspeereena*
blood	sangue *sangway*
broken	rotto *rotto*
casualty (department)	pronto soccorso *pronto sokorso*
chemist's	farmacia *farmacheea*
condom	preservativo *prayzervatteevo*
dentist	dentista *denteesta*
diarrhoea	diarrea *dee-aray-a*
doctor	medico *maydeeko*
food poisoning	intossicazione alimentare *eentosseekatsee-onay alleementaray*
GP	medico generico *maydeeko jaynayreeko*
gynaecologist	ginecologo *jeenaykologo*
hospital	ospedale *ospaydalay*
infection	infezione *eenfetsee-onay*

medicine	medicina *maydeecheena*
painkiller	analgesico *annaljayzeeko*
periods	mestruazioni *mestroo-atsee-onee*
plaster	cerotto *chayroto*
rash	eruzione cutanea *ayrootsee-onay kootannay-a*
spot	brufolo *broofolo*
sunburn	eritema solare *ayreetayma solaray*
surgical spirit	alcol denaturato *alkol daynatoorato*
tablet	compressa *kompressa*
temperature	febbre *febray*
vaccination	vaccino *vacheeno*
x-ray	radiografia *radee-ograffee-a*
to disinfect	disinfettare *deezeenfettaray*
to faint	svenire *zvayneeray*
to vomit	vomitare *vomeetaray*

Expressing yourself

does anyone have an aspirin/a tampon/a plaster, by any chance?
qualcuno per caso ha un'aspirina/un assorbente interno/un cerotto?
kwalkoono per kazo a oonaspeereena/oon assorbentay intayrno/oon chayroto?

I need to see a doctor
devo andare da un medico
dayvo andaray da oon maydeeko

where can I find a doctor?
dove posso trovare un medico?
dovay posso trovaray oon maydeeko?

as soon as possible
il più presto possibile
eel pyoo presto posseebeelay

no, it doesn't matter
no, non importa
no, non eemporta

I'd like to make an appointment for today
vorrei prendere appuntamento per oggi
voray-ee prenderay apoontammento per ojee

can you send an ambulance to …
può mandare un'ambulanza in …
poo-o mandaray oonamboolantsa een …

I've broken my glasses
ho rotto i miei occhiali
o rotto ee mee-ay-ee okee-allee

I've lost a contact lens
ho perso una lente a contatto
o perso oona lentay a kontato

Understanding

pronto soccorso	casualty department
ricetta	prescription
studio medico	doctor's surgery

non c'è posto fino a giovedì
there are no available appointments until Thursday

va bene venerdì alle due?
is Friday at 2pm OK?

AT THE DOCTOR'S OR THE HOSPITAL

Expressing yourself

I have an appointment with Dr ...
ho un appuntamento con il Dottor ...
o oon apootammento kon eel dotor ...

I don't feel very well
non mi sento bene
non mee sento baynay

I feel very weak
mi sento molto debole
mee sento molto daybolay

I don't know what it is
non so cosa sia
non so koza see-a

I've been bitten/stung by ...
mi ha morso/punto ...
mee a morso/poonto

I've got a headache
ho mal di testa
o mal dee testa

I've got toothache/stomachache
ho mal di denti/mal di pancia
o mal dee dentee/mal dee pancha

I've got a sore throat
mi fa male la gola
mee fa mallay la gola

it hurts
mi fa male
mee fa mallay

I feel sick
ho la nausea
o la nowzay-a

it's been three days
è da tre giorni
ay da tray jornee

I've got a temperature
ho la febbre
o la febray

I have a heart condition
soffro di cuore
sofro dee coo-oray

I'm on the pill/the minipill
prendo la pillola/la minipillola
prendo la peelola/la meeneepeelola

I've twisted my ankle
ho preso una storta
o prayzo oona storta

I've had a blackout
ho perso i sensi
o perso ee sensee

is it serious?
è grave?
ay gravay?

how is he/she?
come sta?
comay sta?

my back hurts
ho mal di schiena
o mal dee skee-ayna

it hurts here
mi fa male qui
mee fa mallay kwee

it's got worse
è peggiorato
ay pejorato

it started last night
è cominciato la notte scorsa
ay komeenchato la notay skorsa

I have asthma
soffro d'asma
sofro dazma

it itches
mi prude
mee prooday

I'm ... months pregnant
sono incinta di ... mesi
sono eencheenta dee ... mayzee

I'm allergic to penicillin
sono allergico alla penicillina
sono allerjeeko alla payneecheeleena

I've lost a filling
mi è saltata un'otturazione
mee ay saltata oonotooratsee-onay

is it contagious?
è contagioso?
ay kontajozo?

how much do I owe you?
quanto le devo?
kwanto lay dayvo?

I fell and hurt my back
mi sono fatto male alla schiena cadendo
mee sono fato mallay alla skee-ayna kadendo

it's never happened to me before
non mi era mai successo prima d'ora
non mee ayra ma-ee soochesso preema dora

**I've been on antibiotics for a week and I'm not getting any
 better**
sono sotto antibiotici da una settimana e non c'è nessun miglioramento
*sono soto anteebee-oteechee da oona setteemana ay non chay nessoon
 meelyoramento*

Understanding

dove le fa male?
where does it hurt?

si sdrai, per favore
lie down, please

è allergico a …?
are you allergic to …?

deve subire un intervento
you're going to need an operation

si accomodi in sala d'attesa
if you'd like to take a seat in the waiting room

è vaccinato contro …?
have you been vaccinated against …?

sta prendendo altri medicinali?
are you taking any other medication?

dovrebbe passare tra qualche giorno
it should clear up in a few days

dovrebbe cicatrizzarsi rapidamente
it should heal quickly

faccia un respiro profondo
take a deep breath

le fa male quando premo qui?
does it hurt when I press here?

le faccio una ricetta
I'm going to write you a prescription

ritorni tra una settimana
come back and see me in a week

HEALTH

103

AT THE CHEMIST'S

Expressing yourself

I'd like a box of plasters, please
vorrei una scatola di cerotti, per favore
voray-ee oona skatola dee chayrotee, per favoray

could I have something for a bad cold?
potrei avere qualcosa per un forte raffreddore?
potray-ee avayray kwalkoza per oon fortay rafredore?

I need something for a cough
ho bisogno di qualcosa contro la tosse
o beezonyo dee kwalkoza kontro la tossay

I'm allergic to aspirin
sono allergico all'aspirina
sono allerjeeko allaspeereena

I need the morning-after pill
ho bisogno della pillola del giorno dopo
o beezonyo della peelola del jorno dopo

I'd like to try a homeopathic remedy
vorrei provare una cura omeopatica
voray-ee provaray oona koora omay-opatteeka

I'd like a bottle of solution for soft contact lenses
vorrei un flacone di soluzione per lenti a contatto morbide
voray-ee oon flakonay dee solootsee-onay per lentee a kontato morbeeday

Understanding

applicare	apply
capsula	capsule
compressa	tablet
controindicazioni	contra-indications
crema	cream
effetti collaterali	possible side effects
polverina	powder

pomata ointment
sciroppo syrup
solo su ricetta medica available on prescription only
supposte suppositories

da prendere tre volte al giorno prima dei pasti
take three times a day before meals

PROBLEMS AND EMERGENCIES

Italy has two police forces: the **polizia** (state police) and the **carabinieri** (military police). They have slightly different responsibilities, but if you have a problem or emergency, either will be able to help you.

In an emergency, dial 113 for the police, 112 for the **carabinieri**, and 115 for the fire brigade (**pompieri**), and in a medical emergency, dial 118 for an ambulance.

The basics

accident	incidente *eencheedentay*
ambulance	ambulanza *amboolantsa*
broken	rotto *rotto*
coastguard	guardia costiera *gwardee-a costee-ayra*
disabled	disabile *deezabbeelay*
doctor	medico *maydeeko*
emergency	emergenza *aymergentsa*
fire brigade	pompieri *pompee-ayree*
fire	incendio *eenchendee-o*
hospital	ospedale *ospaydalay*
ill	malato *malato*
injured	ferito *fayreeto*
late	in ritardo *een reetardo*
police	polizia *poleetsee-a*

Expressing yourself

can you help me?
mi può aiutare?
mee poo-o a-yootaray?

help!
aiuto!
a- yooto!

fire!
al fuoco!
al foo-oko!

be careful!
attenzione!
attentsee-onay!

it's an emergency!
è un'emergenza!
ay oonaymergentsa!

there's been an accident
c'è stato un incidente
chay stato oon eencheedentay

I've lost …
ho perso …
o perso …

I've been attacked
sono stato aggredito
sono stato agraydeeto

what do I have to do?
cosa devo fare?
koza dayvo faray?

my bag's been snatched
mi hanno scippato la borsa
mee ano sheepato la borsa

could I borrow your phone, please?
mi può prestare il suo telefono, per favore?
mee poo-o prestaray eel soo-o taylayfono, per favoray?

does anyone here speak English?
c'è qualcuno qui che parla inglese?
chay kwalkoono kwee kay parla eenglayzay?

I need to contact the British consulate
devo contattare il consolato britannico
dayvo kontataray eel konsoolato breetanneeko

where's the nearest police station?
dov'è il commissariato più vicino?
dovay eel comeesaree-ato pyoo veecheeno?

my passport/credit card has been stolen
mi hanno rubato il passaporto/la carta di credito
mee ano roobato eel passaporto/la karta dee craydeeto

my son/daughter is missing
mio figlio è sparito/mia figlia è sparita
mee-o feelyo ay sparreeto/mee-a feelya ay sparreeta

my car's been towed away
mi hanno portato la macchina al deposito
mee ano portato la makeena al daypozeeto

my car's been broken into
mi hanno forzato la portiera della macchina
mee ano fortsato la portee-ayra della makeena

I've broken down
sono rimasto in panne
sono reemasto een pannay

there's a man following me
c'è un uomo che mi segue
chay oon oo-omo kay mee saygway

he's drowning, get help!
sta annegando, cercate aiuto!
sta annaygando, cherkatay a-yooto!

is there disabled access?
c'è un accesso per i disabili?
chay oon achesso per ee deezabeelee?

can you keep an eye on my things for a minute?
può dare un'occhiata alla mia roba un attimo?
poo-o daray oonokee-ata alla mee-a roba oon atteemo?

Understanding

attenti al cane	beware of the dog
fuori servizio	out of order
pronto intervento	police emergency services
soccorso alpino	mountain rescue
soccorso stradale	breakdown service
ufficio oggetti smarriti	lost property
uscita d'emergenza	emergency exit

POLICE

Expressing yourself

I want to report something stolen
vorrei denunciare un furto
voray-ee daynooncharay oon foorto

I need a document from the police for my insurance company
ho bisogno di un certificato di polizia per la mia compagnia di assicurazioni
o beezonyo dee oon cherteefeekato dee poleetsee-a per la mee-a kompanyee-a dee asseekooratsee-onee

Understanding

Filling in forms

cognome	surname
nome	first name
indirizzo	address
codice postale	postcode
paese	country
nazionalità	nationality
data di nascita	date of birth
luogo di nascita	place of birth
età	age
sesso	sex
durata del soggiorno	duration of stay
data d'arrivo/di partenza	arrival/departure date
passaporto numero	passport number
professione	occupation

può aprire questa borsa, per favore?
would you open this bag, please?

può compilare questo modulo, per favore?
would you fill in this form, please?

cosa manca?
what's missing?

quando è successo?
when did this happen?

dove alloggia?
where are you staying?

può descriverlo/descriverla?
can you describe him/her/it?

può firmare qui, per favore?
would you sign here, please?

Some informal expressions

la galera the nick
farsi beccare dalla polizia to get nicked by the police
fregare qualcosa to pinch something

TIME AND DATE

The basics

after	dopo *dopo*
already	già *ja*
always	sempre *sempray*
at lunchtime	a pranzo *a prandzo*
at the beginning/ end of	all'inizio/alla fine di *alleeneetsee-o/alla feenay dee*
at the moment	attualmente *attoo-almentay*
before	prima *preema*
between ... and ...	tra ... e ... *tra ... ay ...*
day	giorno *jorno*
during	durante *doorantay*
early	presto *presto*
evening	sera *sayra*
for a long time	per molto tempo *per molto tempo*
from ... to ...	da ... a ... *da ... a ...*
from time to time	ogni tanto *onyee tanto*
in a little while	tra poco *tra poko*
in the evening	di sera *dee sayra*
in the middle of	a metà ... *a mayta*
last	ultimo *oolteemo*
late	tardi *tardee*
midday	mezzogiorno *medzojorno*
midnight	mezzanotte *medzanottay*
morning	mattino *matteeno*
month	mese *mayzay*
never	mai *ma-ee*
next	prossimo *prosseemo*
night	notte *nottay*
not yet	non ancora *non ankora*
now	ora *ora*
occasionally	occasionalmente *okazee-onalmentay*
often	spesso *spesso*
rarely	raramente *raramentay*
recently	recentemente *raychentaymentay*

since	da *da*
sometimes	a volte *a voltay*
soon	presto *presto*
still	ancora *ankora*
straightaway	subito *soobeeto*
until	fino a *feeno a*
week	settimana *setteemana*
weekend	fine settimana *feenay setteemana*
year	anno *anno*

Expressing yourself

see you soon!
a presto!
a presto!

see you later!
a dopo!
a dopo!

see you on Monday!
a lunedì!
a loonaydee!

have a good weekend!
buon fine settimana!
boo-on feenay setteemana!

sorry I'm late
scusa, sono in ritardo
skooza, sono een reetardo

I haven't been there yet
non ci sono ancora stato
non chee sono ankora stato

I haven't had time to …
non ho avuto il tempo di …
non o avooto eel tempo dee …

I've got plenty of time
ho molto tempo
o molto tempo

I'm in a rush
ho fretta
o fretta

hurry up!
sbrigati!
zbreegattee!

just a minute, please
un attimo, per favore
oon atteemo, per favoray

I had a late night
sono andato a letto tardi
sono andato a letto tardi

I got up very early
mi sono alzato molto presto
mee sono altsato molto presto

I waited ages
ho aspettato per ore
o aspettato per oray

I have to get up very early tomorrow to catch my plane
devo alzarmi molto presto domani per prendere l'aereo
dayvo altsarmee molto presto domannee per prendayray la-ayray-o

we only have 4 days left
ci restano solo quattro giorni
chee restano solo kwatro jornee

THE DATE

How to express dates:

In Italian, the year is preceded by an article. So "in June 2006" is translated as **nel giugno del 2006**, "in '99" is **nel '99** and "from 2005 to 2006" is **dal 2005 al 2006**.

There are two ways to express the century, starting from the 11th century: "the 15th century" can either be **il quindicesimo secolo** or **il Quattrocento**.

The basics

... ago	... fa *... fa*
in two days' time	tra due giorni *tra doo-ay jornee*
last night	la notte scorsa *la nottay skorsa*
the day after tomorrow	dopodomani *dopodomannee*
the day before yesterday	l'altroieri *laltro-ee-ayree*
today	oggi *ojee*
tomorrow	domani *domannee*
tomorrow morning/ afternoon/evening	domani mattina/pomeriggio/sera *domannee matteena/pomayreejo/sayra*
yesterday	ieri *ee-ayree*
yesterday morning/ afternoon/evening	ieri mattina/pomeriggio/sera *ee-ayree matteena/pomayreejo/sayra*

Expressing yourself

I was born in …
sono nato nel …
sono nato nel …

I came here a few years ago
sono venuto qui qualche anno fa
sono vaynooto kwee kwalkay anno fa

I spent a month in Italy last summer
ho passato un mese in Italia l'estate scorsa
o passato oon mayzay een eetalee-a lestatay skorsa

I was here last year at the same time
sono venuto qui l'anno scorso nello stesso periodo
sono vaynooto kwee lanno skorso nello stesso periodo

what's the date today?
quanti ne abbiamo oggi?
kwantee nay abbee-amo ojee?

what day is it today?
che giorno è oggi?
kay jorno ay ojee?

it's the 1st of May
è il primo maggio
ay eel preemo majo

I'm staying until Sunday
mi fermo fino a domenica
mee fermo feeno a domayneeka

we're leaving tomorrow
partiamo domani
partee-amo domannee

I already have plans for Tuesday
ho già qualcosa in programma per martedì
o ja kwalkoza een programma per martaydee

Understanding

due volte
tutti i giorni
tutti i lunedì

twice
every day
every Monday

TIME AND DATE

tre volte all'ora/al giorno	three times an hour/a day
una volta	once

è stato costruito a metà del diciannovesimo secolo
it was built in the mid-nineteenth century

c'è molta gente qui d'estate
it gets very busy here in the summer

quando parti?
when are you leaving?

quanto ti fermi?
how long are you staying?

THE TIME

Italians tend to use the 24-hour clock more than we do in the UK, though in ordinary conversation they still use the 12-hour clock. For example, 2 pm is written as 2 or, in more official contexts, as **14.00**, and spoken as **le due (del pomeriggio)** or **le quattordici** respectively.

The basics

half an hour	mezzora *medzora*
in the afternoon	del pomeriggio *del pomayreejo*
in the morning	del mattino *del matteeno*
midday	mezzogiorno *medzojorno*
midnight	mezzanotte *medzanottay*
on time	puntuale *poontoo-alay*
quarter of an hour	quarto d'ora *kwarto dora*
three quarters of an hour	tre quarti d'ora *tray kwartee dora*

Expressing yourself

excuse me, have you got the time, please?
mi scusi, ha l'ora, per favore?
mee skoozee, a lora, per favoray?

what time is it?
che ora è?
kay ora ay?

it's nearly one o'clock
è quasi l'una
ay kwazee loona

it's a quarter past one
è l'una e un quarto
ay loona ay oon kwarto

it's twenty past twelve
sono le dodici e venti
sono lay dodeechee ay ventee

it's half past one
è l'una e mezza
ay loona ay medza

it's exactly three o'clock
sono esattamente le tre
sono ayzatamentay lay tray

it's ten past one
è l'una e dieci
ay loona ay dee-aychee

it's a quarter to one
è l'una meno un quarto
ay loona mayno oon kwarto

it's twenty to twelve
sono le dodici meno venti
sono lay dodeechee mayno ventee

I arrived at about two o'clock
sono arrivato intorno alle due
sono arreevato eentorno allay doo-ay

I set my alarm for nine
ho messo la sveglia alle nove
o messo la svelya allay novay

I waited twenty minutes
ho aspettato venti minuti
o aspetato ventee meenootee

I got home an hour ago
sono arrivato a casa un'ora fa
sono arreevato a kaza oonora fa

shall we meet in half an hour?
ci vediamo tra mezzora?
chee vaydee-amo tra medzora?

the train was fifteen minutes late
il treno aveva quindici minuti di ritardo
eel trayno avayva kweendeechee meenootee dee reetardo

I'll be back in a quarter of an hour
torno tra un quarto d'ora
torno tra oon kwarto dora

there's a three-hour time difference between … and …
ci sono tre ore di fuso orario tra … e …
chee sono tray oray dee foozo oraree-o tra … ay …

Understanding

aperto dalle dieci alle sedici
open from 10am to 4pm

lo danno tutte le sere alle sette
it's on every evening at seven

partenze ogni mezzora
departs on the hour and the half-hour

dura circa un'ora e mezza
it lasts around an hour and a half

apre alle dieci del mattino
it opens at ten in the morning

Some informal expressions

alle otto e passa well past eight
alle otto spaccate at eight on the dot
sono secoli che … it's ages since …

NUMBERS

Numbers with decimals are written with a comma and not with a full stop as in English, ie 2,5 in Italian = 2.5 in English. When giving prices, **1,30 euro** is pronounced **un euro e trenta**. When writing thousands, Italian uses a full stop and not a comma as in English, ie 100.000 in Italian = 100,000 in English.

0	zero *dzayro*
1	uno *oono*
2	due *doo-ay*
3	tre *tray*
4	quattro *kwatro*
5	cinque *cheenkway*
6	sei *say-ee*
7	sette *settay*
8	otto *otto*
9	nove *novay*
10	dieci *dee-aychee*
11	undici *oondeechee*
12	dodici *dodeechee*
13	tredici *traydeechee*
14	quattordici *kwatordeechee*
15	quindici *kweendeechee*
16	sedici *saydeechee*
17	diciassette *deechassettee*
18	diciotto *deechotto*
19	diciannove *deechanovay*
20	venti *ventee*
21	ventuno *ventoono*
22	ventidue *venteedoo-ay*
30	trenta *trenta*
35	trentacinque *trentacheenkway*
40	quaranta *kwaranta*
50	cinquanta *cheenkwanta*

60	**sessanta** *sessanta*
70	**settanta** *setanta*
80	**ottanta** *otanta*
90	**novanta** *novanta*
100	**cento** *chento*
101	**centouno** *chento-oono*
200	**duecento** *doo-aychento*
500	**cinquecento** *cheenkwaychento*
1 000	**mille** *meelay*
2 000	**duemila** *doo-aymeela*
10 000	**diecimila** *dee-aycheemeela*
1 000 000	**un milione** *oon meelee-onay*

first	**primo** *preemo*
second	**secondo** *saykondo*
third	**terzo** *tertso*
fourth	**quarto** *kwarto*
fifth	**quinto** *kweento*
sixth	**sesto** *sesto*
seventh	**settimo** *setteemo*
eighth	**ottavo** *otavo*
ninth	**nono** *nono*
tenth	**decimo** *daycheemo*
twentieth	**ventesimo** *ventayzeemo*

20 plus 3 equals 23
venti più tre uguale ventitré
ventee pyoo tray oogoo-alay ventitray

20 minus 3 equals 17
venti meno tre uguale diciassette
ventee mayno tray oogoo-alay deechassettay

20 multiplied by 4 equals 80
venti per quattro uguale ottanta
ventee per kwatro oogoo-alay otanta

20 divided by 4 equals 5
venti diviso quattro uguale cinque
ventee deeveezo kwatro oogoo-alay cheenkway

NUMBERS

DICTIONARY

ENGLISH-ITALIAN

A

a un(o), una
abbey abbazia *f*
able: to be able to potere
about circa; **to be about to do** stare per fare
above sopra
abroad all'estero
accept accettare
access accesso *m* 108
accident incidente *m* 30, 107
accommodation sistemazione *f*
across attraverso
adaptor adattatore *m*
address indirizzo *m*
admission ingresso *m*
advance: in advance in anticipo 60
advice consigli *mpl*; **to ask someone's advice** chiedere consiglio a qualcuno
advise consigliare
aeroplane aeroplano *m*
after dopo
afternoon pomeriggio *m*
after-sun (cream) doposole *m*
again di nuovo
against contro
age età *f*
air aria *f*
air conditioning aria *f* condizionata
airline compagnia *f* aerea

airmail via aerea
airport aeroporto *m*
alarm clock sveglia *f*
alcohol alcol *m*
alive vivo
all tutto; **all day** tutto il giorno; **all week** tutta la settimana; **all the better** molto meglio; **all the same** comunque; **all the time** tutto il tempo; **all inclusive** tutto compreso
allergic allergico 102, 104
almost quasi
already già
also anche
although nonostante
always sempre
ambulance ambulanza *f* 100
American *(adj)* americano
American *(n) (person)* americano *m*, americana *f*
among tra
anaesthetic anestesia *f*
and e
animal animale *m*
ankle caviglia *f*
anniversary anniversario *m*
another un altro *m*, un'altra *f*
answer *(n)* risposta *f*
answer *(v)* rispondere
answering machine segreteria *f* telefonica

ant formica *f*
antibiotics antibiotici *mpl*
anybody, anyone chiunque
anything qualsiasi cosa
anyway comunque
appendicitis appendicite *f*
appointment appuntamento *m*; **to make an appointment** prendere (un) appuntamento **100**; **to have an appointment (with)** avere un appuntamento (con) **101**
April aprile *m*
area zona *f*; **in the area** in zona
arm braccio *m*
around intorno a
arrange organizzare; **to arrange to meet** combinare di incontrarsi
arrival arrivo *m*
arrive arrivare
art arte *f*
artist artista *mf*
as come; **as soon as possible** il prima possibile; **as soon as** (non) appena; **as well as** (così) come
ashtray portacenere *m*
ask chiedere; **to ask a question** fare una domanda
aspirin aspirina *f*
asthma asma *f* **102**
at a
attack *(v)* aggredire **107**
August agosto *m*
autumn autunno *m*
available disponibile
avenue viale *m*
away: 10 miles away a 10 miglia

B

baby bambino *m* (piccolo), bambina *f* (piccola)
baby's bottle biberon *m*
back schiena *f*; **at the back of** in fondo a
backpack zaino *m*
bad cattivo; **it's not bad** non è male
bag borsa *f*
baggage bagagli *mpl*
bake cuocere (in forno)
baker's panetteria *f*
balcony balcone *m*
bandage benda *f*
bank banca *f* **88**
banknote banconota *f*
bar bar *m*
barbecue barbecue *m*
bath (vasca da) bagno *m*; **to have a bath** fare il bagno
bath towel asciugamano *m* da bagno
bathroom bagno *m*
battery batteria *f* **30**
be essere
beach spiaggia *f*
beach umbrella ombrellone *m*
beard barba *f*
beautiful bello
because perché; **because of** a causa di
bed letto *m*
bee ape *f*
before prima
begin iniziare
beginner principiante *mf*

beginning inizio m; **at the beginning** all'inizio
behind dietro
Belgian *(adj) (person)* belga
Belgian *(n)* belga mf
Belgium Belgio m
believe credere
below sotto
beside accanto a
best migliore; **the best** il (la) migliore
better migliore; **to get better** migliorare; **it's better to …** è meglio …
better *(adv)* meglio
bicycle bicicletta f
bicycle pump pompa f da bicicletta
big grande
bike bici f
bill conto m **47**, **48**
bin bidone m (della spazzatura)
binoculars binocolo m
birthday compleanno m
bit pezzo m
bite *(n)* morso m
bite *(v)* mordere
black nero
blackout svenimento m
blanket coperta f
bleed sanguinare
bless: bless you! salute!
blind cieco
blister vescica f
blood sangue m
blood pressure pressione f sanguigna
blue blu
board imbarcarsi **24**
boarding imbarco m

boat barca f
body corpo m
book *(n)* libro m; **book of tickets** carnet m di biglietti
book *(v)* prenotare **60**
bookshop libreria f
boot *(knee-length)* stivale m; *(for hiking)* scarpone m; *(of car)* portabagagli m
borrow prendere in prestito
botanical garden giardino m botanico
both entrambi; **both of us** tutti e due
bottle bottiglia f **45**
bottle opener apribottiglie m
bottom fondo m; **at the bottom** in fondo; **at the bottom of** in fondo a
bowl scodella f
bra reggiseno m
brake *(n)* freno m
brake *(v)* frenare
bread pane m
break rompere; **to break one's leg** rompersi una gamba
break down rompersi **30**, **108**
breakdown guasto m
breakdown service soccorso m stradale
breakfast *(prima)* colazione f **35**, **36**; **to have breakfast** fare colazione
bridge ponte m
bring portare
brochure dépliant m
broken rotto
bronchitis bronchite f
brother fratello m

brown marrone
brush spazzola *f*
build costruire
building edificio *m*
bump bernoccolo *m*
bumper paraurti *m*
buoy boa *f*
burn *(n)* bruciatura *f*
burn *(v)* bruciare; **to burn oneself** bruciarsi
burst *(v)* scoppiare
burst *(adj)* scoppiato
bus autobus *m* **28**
bus route linea *f* dell'autobus
bus station stazione *f* degli autobus
bus stop fermata *f* dell'autobus
busy *(person)* occupato; *(place)* affollato
but ma
butcher's macelleria *f*
buy comprare **80**
by da; **by car** in macchina
bye! arrivederci!

C

café caffè *m*
call *(n)* chiamata *f*
call *(v)* chiamare **96**; **to be called** chiamarsi
call back richiamare **96**
camera macchina *f* fotografica
camper *(person)* campeggiatore *m*, campeggiatrice *f*; *(van)* camper *m*
camping campeggio *m*; **to go camping** andare in campeggio
camping stove fornello *m* da campeggio

campsite campeggio *m* **39**
can *(n) (for liquid)* lattina *f*; *(for food)* scatola *f*
can *(v)* potere; **I can't** non posso
can opener apriscatole *m*
cancel annullare
candle candela *f*
car macchina *f*
car park parcheggio *m*
caravan roulotte *f*
card tessera *f*
carry portare
case: in case of ... in caso di ...
cash contanti *mpl*; **to pay cash** pagare in contanti **79**
cashpoint bancomat® *m* **88**, **89**
castle castello *m*
catch prendere
cathedral cattedrale *f*
CD cd *m*
cemetery cimitero *m*
centimetre centimetro *m*
centre centro *m* **36**
century secolo *m*
chair sedia *f*
chairlift seggiovia *f*
change *(n)* cambio *m*; *(money)* resto *m* **78**
change *(v)* cambiare **88**, **89**
changing room *(in shop)* cabina *f* di prova **82**; *(at swimming pool, gym)* spogliatoio *m*
channel canale *m*
chapel cappella *f*
charge *(n)* costo *m*
charge *(v) (amount)* far pagare; *(battery, mobile)* caricare
cheap economico
check verificare

check in *(v)* fare il check-in
check-in *(n)* check-in *m* **24**
checkout cassa *f*
cheers! cincin!
chemist's farmacia *f*
cheque assegno *m*
chest petto *m*
child bambino *m*, bambina *f*
chilly freddo
chimney camino *m*
chin mento *m*
chocolate cioccolato *m*
church chiesa *f*
cigar sigaro *m*
cigarette sigaretta *f*
cigarette paper cartine *fpl* (per sigarette)
cinema cinema *m*
circus circo *m*
city città *f*
clean *(adj)* pulito
clean *(v)* pulire
cliff scogliera *f*
climate clima *m*
climbing alpinismo *m*
cloakroom guardaroba *m*
close *(v)* chiudere
closed chiuso
closing time ora *f* di chiusura
clothes abiti *mpl*, abbigliamento *m*
club discoteca *f*
clutch frizione *f*
coach pullman *m* **28**
coast costa *f*
coathanger attaccapanni *m*
cockroach scarafaggio *m*
coffee caffè *m* **46**
coil *(contraceptive)* spirale *f*
coin moneta *f*

Coke® Coca-Cola® *f*
cold *(n)* raffreddore *m*; **to have a cold** avere il raffreddore
cold *(adj)* freddo; **it's cold** fa freddo; **I'm cold** ho freddo
collection collezione *f*
colour colore *m*
comb pettine *m*
come venire
come back ritornare
come in entrare
come out uscire
comfortable comodo
company società *f*
compartment scompartimento *m*
complain lamentarsi
comprehensive insurance assicurazione *f* kasko **30**
computer computer *m*
concert concerto *m* **60**
concert hall sala *f* concerti
concession sconto *m* **23**, **66**
condom preservativo *m*
confirm confermare **25**
connection coincidenza *f* **25**
constipated stitico
consulate consolato *m* **107**
contact *(n)* contatto *m*
contact *(v)* contattare **107**
contact lenses lenti *fpl* a contatto
contagious contagioso
contraceptive contraccettivo *m*
cook cucinare
cooked cotto
cooking cucina *f*; **to do the cooking** cucinare
cool fresco
corkscrew cavatappi *m*
correct giusto

cost (n) costo m
cost (v) costare
cotton cotone m
cotton bud cotton fioc® m
cotton wool ovatta f
cough (n) tosse f; **to have a cough** avere la tosse
cough (v) tossire
count contare
country paese m
countryside campagna f
course: of course certo
cover (n) (for bed) coperta f; (of book, magazine) copertina f
cover (v) coprire
credit card carta f di credito **34, 47, 79, 89**
cross (n) croce f
cross (v) attraversare
cruise crociera f
cry piangere
cup tazza f
currency valuta f
customs dogana f
cut tagliare; **to cut oneself** tagliarsi
cycle path pista f ciclabile **73**

D

damaged danneggiato
damp umido
dance (n) ballo m
dance (v) ballare
dangerous pericoloso
dark scuro; **dark blue** blu m scuro
date (n) data f; **out of date** superato
date from risalire a

date of birth data f di nascita
daughter figlia f
day giorno m; **the day after tomorrow** dopodomani; **the day before yesterday** l'altroieri
dead morto; (battery) scarico
deaf sordo
dear caro
debit card bancomat® m
December dicembre m
declare dichiarare
deep profondo
degree grado m
delay ritardo m
delayed in ritardo
deli gastronomia f
dentist dentista mf
deodorant deodorante m
department reparto m
department store grande magazzino m
departure partenza f
depend: that depends (on) dipende (da)
deposit cauzione f
dessert dolce m **45**
develop: to get a film developed far sviluppare un rullino **86**
diabetes diabete m
dialling code prefisso m (telefonico)
diarrhoea: to have diarrhoea avere la diarrea
die morire
diesel diesel m
diet dieta f; **to be on a diet** essere a dieta
different (from) diverso (da)

difficult difficile
digital camera macchina *f* fotografica digitale
dinner cena *f*; **to have dinner** cenare
direct diretto
direction direzione *f*; **to have a good sense of direction** avere il senso dell'orientamento
directory elenco *m* telefonico
directory enquiries ricerca *f* elenco abbonati
dirty *(adj)* sporco
disabled disabile **108**
disaster disastro *m*
discount sconto *m* **66**; **to give someone a discount** fare uno sconto a qualcuno
dish piatto *m*; **dish of the day** piatto del giorno
dishes piatti *mpl*; **to do the dishes** lavare i piatti
dish towel strofinaccio *m* da cucina
dishwasher lavastoviglie *f*
disinfect disinfettare
disposable usa e getta
disturb disturbare; **do not disturb** non disturbare
dive tuffarsi
diving: to go diving fare immersioni
do fare; **do you have a light?** ha da accendere?
doctor medico *m* **100**
door porta *f*
door code codice *m* apriporta
downstairs di sotto
draught beer birra *f* alla spina

dress: to get dressed vestirsi
dressing condimento *m*
drink *(n)* bevanda *f*; **to go for a drink** andare a bere qualcosa **43**, **58**; **to have a drink** bere qualcosa
drink *(v)* bere
drinking water acqua *f* potabile
drive: *(n)* **to go for a drive** fare un giro in macchina
drive *(v)* guidare
driving licence patente *f* (di guida)
drops gocce *fpl*
drown annegare
drugs droga *f*
drunk ubriaco
dry *(adj)* asciutto
dry *(v)* asciugare
dry cleaner's lavanderia *f* (a secco)
duck anatra *f*
during durante; **during the week** durante la settimana
dustbin pattumiera *f*
duty chemist farmacia *f* di turno

E

each ogni; **each one** ognuno
ear orecchio *m*
early presto
earplugs tappi *mpl* per le orecchie
earrings orecchini *mpl*
earth terra *f*
east est; **in the east** a est; **(to the) east of** a est di
Easter Pasqua *f*
easy facile
eat mangiare **42**
economy class classe *f* economica

Elastoplast® cerotto *m*
electric elettrico
electric shaver rasoio *m* elettrico
electricity elettricità *f*
electricity meter contatore *m* della luce
e-mail e-mail *f*
e-mail address indirizzo *m* e-mail **17, 92**
embassy ambasciata *f*
emergency emergenza *f* **107**; **in an emergency** in caso di emergenza
emergency exit uscita *f* di sicurezza
empty vuoto
end fine *f*; **at the end of** alla fine di; **at the end of the street** in fondo alla strada
engaged occupato
engine motore *m*
England Inghilterra *f*
English *(adj)* inglese
English *(n) (language)* inglese *m*; **the English** *(people)* gli inglesi
enjoy: enjoy your meal! buon appetito!; **to enjoy oneself** divertirsi
enough abbastanza; **that's enough** basta
entrance ingresso *m*
envelope busta *f*
epileptic epilettico
equipment attrezzatura *f*
espresso caffè *m* (espresso)
euro euro *m*
Eurocheque eurocheque *m*
Europe Europa *f*
European europeo

evening sera *f*; **in the evening** di sera
every ogni; **every day** ogni giorno
everybody, everyone tutti
everywhere dappertutto
except tranne
exceptional eccezionale
excess eccedenza *f*
exchange cambio *m*
exchange rate tasso *m* di cambio
excuse *(n)* scusa *f*
excuse *(v):* **excuse me** mi scusi
exhaust tubo *m* di scappamento
exhausted sfinito
exhaust pipe tubo *m* di scappamento
exhibition mostra *f* **66**
exit uscita *f*
expensive caro
expiry date data *f* di scadenza
express *(adj)* espresso
extra extra
eye occhio *m*

F

face faccia *f*
facecloth guanto *m* di spugna
fact fatto *m*; **in fact** in realtà
faint svenire
fair *(n)* fiera *f*
fair *(adj)* giusto
fall *(v)* cadere; **to fall asleep** addormentarsi; **to fall ill** ammalarsi
family famiglia *f*
fan *(electric)* ventilatore *m*; *(person)* patito *m*, patita *f*
far lontano; **far from** lontano da
fare tariffa *f*

fast rapido
fast-food restaurant fast food *m*
fat *(adj)* grasso
father padre *m*
favour favore *m*; **to do someone a favour** fare un favore a qualcuno
favourite preferito
fax fax *m*
February febbraio *m*
fed up (with) stufo (di)
feel sentire **101**; **to feel good/ bad** sentirsi bene/male
feeling *(physical)* sensazione *f*; *(emotional)* sentimento *m*
ferry traghetto *m*
festival festival *m*
fetch: to go and fetch someone/something andare a prendere qualcuno/qualcosa
fever febbre *f*; **to have a fever** avere la febbre
few pochi
fiancé fidanzato *m*
fiancée fidanzata *f*
fight lottare
fill riempire
fill in compilare
filling *(in tooth)* otturazione *f*
fill out compilare
fill up: to fill up with petrol fare il pieno (di benzina)
film *(for camera)* pellicola *f* **86**; *(movie)* film *m*
finally alla fine
find trovare
fine *(n)* multa *f*
fine *(adj)* ottimo; **I'm fine** sto bene; **it's fine** va bene
finger dito *m*

finish finire
fire fuoco *m*; *(destructive)* incendio *m*; **fire!** al fuoco!
fire brigade pompieri *mpl*
fireworks fuochi *mpl* d'artificio
first primo; **first (of all)** innanzitutto
first class prima classe *f*
first course primo *m*
first floor primo piano *m*
first name nome *m* (di battesimo)
fish *(n)* pesce *m*
fishmonger's pescheria *f*
fish shop pescheria *f*
fitting room camerino *m*
fizzy gasato
flash flash *m*
flask thermos *m*
flat *(adj)* piatto; **flat tyre** gomma *f* a terra
flat *(n)* appartamento *m*
flavour gusto *m*
flaw difetto *m*
flight volo *m*
flip-flops infradito *mpl*
floor pavimento *m*; **on the floor** per terra
flu influenza *f*
fly *(n)* mosca *f*
fly *(v)* volare
food cibo *m*
food poisoning intossicazione *f* alimentare
foot piede *m*
for per; **for an hour** per un'ora
forbidden vietato
forecast previsioni *fpl* (del tempo)
forehead fronte *f*
foreign straniero**

foreigner straniero *m*, straniera *f*
forest foresta *f*
fork forchetta *f*
former ex
forward *(adj)* in avanti
four-star petrol (benzina) super *f*
fracture frattura *f*
fragile fragile
France Francia *f*
free libero; *(for nothing)* gratuito
freezer congelatore *m*
French *(adj)* francese
French *(n) (language)* francese *m*; **the French** *(people)* i francesi
Friday venerdì *m*
fridge frigorifero *m*
fried fritto
friend amico *m*, amica *f*
from da; **from … to …** da … a …
front davanti *m*; **in front of** davanti a
fry friggere
frying pan padella *f*
full pieno; **full of** pieno di
full board pensione *f* completa
full fare tariffa *f* intera
full price prezzo *m* pieno **66**
funfair luna park *m*
fuse fusibile *m*

G

gallery galleria *f*
game partita *f*
garage officina *f* **30**
garden giardino *m*
gas gas *m*
gas cylinder bombola *f* del gas
gastric flu influenza *f* intestinale

gate *(in wall, fence)* cancello *m*; *(at airport)* uscita *f*
gauze voile *f*
gay gay
gearbox scatola *f* del cambio
general generale
gents' (toilet) bagno *m* degli uomini
German *(adj)* tedesco
German *(n) (person)* tedesco *m*, tedesca *f*; *(language)* tedesco *m*
Germany Germania *f*
get ottenere
get off scendere
get up alzarsi
gift wrap carta *f* da regalo
girl ragazza *f*
girlfriend ragazza *f*
give dare
give back restituire
glass bicchiere *m*; **a glass of water/of wine** un bicchiere d'acqua/di vino
glasses occhiali *mpl*
gluten-free senza glutine
go andare; **to go to Rome/to Italy** andare a Roma/in Italia; **we're going home tomorrow** andiamo a casa domani
go away andare via
go in entrare
go out uscire
go with accompagnare
golf golf *m*
golf course campo *m* da golf
good buono; **good morning** buongiorno; **good afternoon** buongiorno; **good evening** buonasera

goodbye arrivederci
goodnight buonanotte
goods merce *f*
GP medico *m* generico
grams grammi *mpl*
grass erba *f*
great ottimo
Great Britain Gran Bretagna *f*
Greece Grecia *f*
Greek *(adj)* greco
Greek *(n) (person)* greco *m*, greca
  f; *(language)* greco *m*
green verde
grey grigio
grocer's fruttivendolo *m*
ground terra *f*; **on the ground**
  per terra
ground floor pianterreno *m*
ground sheet telo *m* impermeabile
  (da mettere per terra)
grow crescere
guarantee garanzia *f*
guest ospite *mf*
guest house pensione *f*
guide guida *f* **60**
guidebook guida *f*
guided tour visita *f* guidata
gynaecologist ginecologo *m*,
  ginecologa *f*

H

hair capelli *mpl*
hairdresser parrucchiere *m*,
  parrucchiera *f*
hairdrier fon *m*
half mezzo; **half a litre/kilo** mezzo
  litro/kilo; **half an hour** mezzora
half-board mezza pensione *f*

half-pint birra *f* piccola
hand mano *f*
handbag borsetta *f*
handbrake freno *m* a mano
handkerchief fazzoletto *m*
hand luggage bagaglio *m* a mano
  25
hand-made fatto a mano
hangover postumi *mpl* di una
  sbornia
happen succedere
happy felice
hard duro
hashish hashish *m*
hat cappello *m*
hate odiare
have avere
have to dovere; **I have to go**
  devo andare
hay fever raffreddore *m* da fieno
he lui
head testa *f*
headache: to have a headache
  avere mal di testa
headlight faro *m*
health salute *f*
hear sentire
heart cuore *m*
heart attack infarto *m*
heat calore *m*
heating riscaldamento *m*
heavy pesante
hello salve; *(on telephone)* pronto
helmet casco *m*
help *(n)* aiuto *m*; **to call for help**
  chiamare aiuto; **help!** aiuto!
help *(v)* aiutare **106**
her *(pron) (direct object)* la;
  (indirect object) le, a lei

her *(adj)* il suo, la sua, i suoi, le sue
here qui; **here is/are** ecco
hers il suo, la sua, i suoi, le sue
herself sé
hi-fi stereo *m*
high alto
high blood pressure pressione *f* (sanguigna) alta
high tide alta marea *f*
hiking escursioni *fpl*; **to go hiking** fare delle escursioni
hill collina *f*
hill-walking escursioni *fpl* in bassa montagna; **to go hill-walking** fare delle escursioni in bassa montagna
him *(direct object)* lo; *(indirect object)* gli, a lui
himself sé
hip fianco *m*
hire *(n)* noleggio *m*
hire *(v)* noleggiare **30**, **70**, **72**, **73**
his il suo, la sua, i suoi, le sue
hitchhike fare l'autostop
hitchhiking autostop *m*
hold tenere
hold on! *(on the phone)* rimanga in linea!
holiday vacanza *f*; **on holiday** in vacanza
holiday camp villaggio *m* turistico
Holland Olanda *f*
home casa *f*; **at home** a casa; **to go home** andare a casa
homosexual omosessuale
honest onesto
honeymoon viaggio *m* di nozze
horse cavallo *m*
hospital ospedale *m*

hot caldo; **it's hot** fa caldo; **hot drink** bevanda *f* calda
hot chocolate cioccolata *f* calda
hotel albergo *m* **36**
hotplate piastra *f* (di cottura)
hour ora *f*; **an hour and a half** un'ora e mezza
house casa *f*
housework lavori *mpl* di casa; **to do the housework** fare i lavori di casa
how come; **how are you?** come va?
hunger fame *f*
hungry: to be hungry avere fame
hurry: to be in a hurry avere fretta
hurry (up) sbrigarsi
hurt: it hurts fa male; **my head hurts** mi fa male la testa
husband marito *m*

I io; **I'm English** sono inglese; **I'm 22 (years old)** ho ventidue anni
ice ghiaccio *m*
ice cube cubetto *m* di ghiaccio
identity card carta *f* d'identità
identity papers documenti *mpl* d'identità
if se
ill malato
illness malattia *f*
important importante
in in; **in England/2006/Italian** in Inghilterra/nel 2006/in italiano; **in the 19th century** nel

diciannovesimo secolo; **in an hour** tra un'ora
included compreso
independent indipendente
indicator freccia *f* (di direzione)
infection infezione *f*
information informazioni *fpl* **65**
injection iniezione *f*
injured ferito
insect insetto *m*
insecticide insetticida *m*
inside dentro
insomnia insonnia *f*
instant coffee caffè *m* solubile
instead invece; **instead of** invece di
insurance assicurazione *f*
intend to... avere intenzione di ...
international internazionale
international money order vaglia *m* internazionale
Internet Internet *m*
Internet café Internet café *m* **92**
invite invitare
Ireland Irlanda *f*
Irish *(adj)* irlandese
Irish *(n) (language)* irlandese *m*; **the Irish** *(people)* gli irlandesi
iron *(n) (metal)* ferro *m*; *(for ironing)* ferro *m* da stiro
iron *(v)* stirare
island isola *f*
it *(direct object)* lo *m*, la *f*; *(indirect object)* gli *m*, le *f*; **it's beautiful** è bello; **it's warm** fa caldo
Italian *(adj)* italiano
Italian *(n) (person)* italiano *m*, italiana *f*; *(language)* italiano *m*

itchy: it's itchy mi prude
item articolo *m*
its il suo, la sua, i suoi, le sue

J

January gennaio *m*
jetlag jetlag *m*
jeweller's gioielleria *f*
jewellery gioielli *mpl*
job lavoro *m*
jogging jogging *m*
journey viaggio *m*
jug *(for wine, water)* caraffa *f*; *(for milk, coffee)* bricco *m*
juice succo *m*
July luglio *m*
jumper maglione *m*
June giugno *m*
just solo; **just before** poco prima; **just a little** solo un po'; **just one** solo uno; **I've just arrived** sono appena arrivato; **just in case** casomai

K

kayak kayak *m*
keep tenere; **to keep doing something** continuare a fare qualcosa; **to keep calm** rimanere calmo
key chiave *f* **30**, **36**, **38**
kidney rene *m*
kill uccidere
kilometre kilometro *m*
kind tipo *m*; **what kind of ...?** che tipo di ...?
kitchen cucina *f*

knee ginocchio *m*
knife coltello *m*
knock down investire
know sapere; **I don't know** non lo so

L

ladies' (toilet) bagno *m* delle donne
lake lago *m*
lamp lampada *f*
landmark punto *m* di riferimento
landscape paesaggio *m*
language lingua *f*
laptop pc *m* portatile
last *(adj)* ultimo; **last year** l'anno scorso
last *(v)* durare
late tardi
late-night opening apertura *f* notturna
laugh ridere
launderette lavanderia *f* automatica
lawyer avvocato *m*
leaflet volantino *m*
leak perdita *f*
learn imparare
least minimo; **at least** almeno
leave partire
left *(n)* sinistra *f*; **to the left (of)** a sinistra (di)
left *(adj)* sinistro
left-luggage (office) deposito *m* bagagli
leg gamba *f*
lend prestare
lens lente *f*

lenses lenti *fpl* (a contatto)
less meno; **less than** meno di
let lasciare; **let's go** andiamo
letter lettera *f*
letterbox buca *f* delle lettere
library biblioteca *f*
life vita *f*
lift ascensore *m*; **to give someone a lift** dare un passaggio a qualcuno
light *(adj)* chiaro; **light green** verde chiaro
light *(n)* luce *f*; **do you have a light?** ha da accendere?
light *(v)* accendere
light bulb lampadina *f*
lighter accendino *m*
lighthouse faro *m*
like *(prep)* come
like: I like dancing mi piace ballare; **I like him** mi piace; **I'd like ...** vorrei ... 18
line linea *f* 27
lip labbro *m*
listen ascoltare; **to listen to someone/something** ascoltare qualcuno/qualcosa
listings magazine rassegna *f* delle manifestazioni
litre litro *m*
little *(adj)* piccolo
little *(adv)* poco; **a little** un po'
live vivere
liver fegato *m*
living room soggiorno *m*
local time ora *f* locale
lock chiudere a chiave
long lungo; **a long time** molto tempo; **how long ...?** quanto (tempo) ...?

look sembrare; **to look tired**
avere l'aria stanca
look after occuparsi di
look at guardare
look for cercare
look like somigliare a
lorry camion *m*
lose perdere **30**; **to get lost**
perdersi; **to be lost** essersi perso
12, **107**
lot: a lot (of) molto; **a lot of**
work molto lavoro; **a lot of**
tourists molti turisti
loud forte
low basso
low blood pressure pressione *f*
(sanguigna) bassa
low-fat light
low tide bassa marea *f*
luck fortuna *f*
lucky fortunato
luggage bagagli *mpl* **25**
lukewarm tiepido
lunch pranzo *m*; **to have lunch**
pranzare
lung polmone *m*
Luxembourg *(city)* Lussemburgo
f; *(country)* Lussemburgo *m*
luxury *(n)* lusso *m*
luxury *(adj)* di lusso

M

magazine rivista *f*
maiden name nome *m* da ragazza
mail posta *f*
main principale
main course secondo *m*
make fare

man uomo *m*
manage cavarsela; **to manage**
to do something riuscire a fare
qualcosa
manager direttore *m*, direttrice *f*
many molti; **how many?** quanti?;
how many times …? quante
volte …?
map cartina *f* **12**, **27**, **65**
March marzo *m*
marina marina *f*
market mercato *m* **80**
married sposato
mass messa *f*
match *(for cigarette)* fiammifero *m*;
(game) partita *f*
material stoffa *f*
matter: it doesn't matter non
importa
mattress materasso *m*
May maggio *m*
maybe forse
me *(direct object)* mi; *(indirect*
object) mi, a me; **me too** anch'io
meal pasto *m*
mean voler dire; **what does …**
mean? cosa vuol dire …?
medicine medicina *f*
medium medio; *(meat)* non
troppo cotto
meet incontrare **59**
meeting riunione *f*
member membro *m*
menu menu *m*
message messaggio *m*
meter contatore *m*
metre metro *m*
microwave forno *m* a microonde
midday mezzogiorno *m*

middle mezzo; **in the middle (of)** in mezzo (a)
midnight mezzanotte *f*
might: it might rain potrebbe piovere
mill mulino *m*
mind: I don't mind per me è lo stesso
mine il mio, la mia, i miei, le mie
mineral water acqua *f* minerale
minister ministro *m*
minute minuto *m*; **at the last minute** all'ultimo minuto
mirror specchio *m*
Miss signorina
miss mancare; **we missed the train** abbiamo perso il treno; **there are two ... missing** mancano due ...
mistake errore *m*; **to make a mistake** fare un errore
mobile (phone) cellulare *m* **95**
modern moderno
moisturizer crema *f* idratante
moment momento *m*; **at the moment** attualmente
monastery monastero *m*
Monday lunedì *m*
money soldi *mpl* **78**
month mese *m*
monument monumento *m*
mood: to be in a good/bad mood essere di buon/cattivo umore
moon luna *f*
moped motorino *m*
more più; **more than** più di; **much more, a lot more** molto di più; **there's no more ...** non c'è più ...

morning mattino *m*
morning-after pill pillola *f* del giorno dopo
mosque moschea *f*
mosquito zanzara *f*
most: the most più; **most people** la maggior parte della gente
mother madre *f*
motorbike moto(cicletta) *f*
motorway autostrada *f*
mountain montagna *f*
mountain bike mountain bike *f*
mountain hut rifugio *m* (di montagna)
mouse *(animal)* topo *m*; *(for computer)* mouse *m*
mouth bocca *f*
movie film *m*
Mr signor
Mrs signora
much: how much? quanto?; **how much is it?, how much does it cost?** quanto costa?
muscle muscolo *m*
museum museo *m*
music musica *f*
must dovere; **it must be 5 o'clock** devono essere le cinque; **I must go** devo andare
my il mio, la mia, i miei, le mie
myself me

nail *(on finger)* unghia *f*; *(metal)* chiodo *m*
naked nudo
name nome *m*; **my name is...** mi chiamo ... **14**

nap sonnellino *m*; **to have a nap** fare un sonnellino

napkin tovagliolo *m*

nappy pannolino *m*

national holiday festa *f* nazionale

nature natura *f*

near vicino; **near the beach** vicino alla spiaggia; **the nearest …** il … più vicino

necessary necessario

neck collo *m*

need aver bisogno di

neighbour vicino *m*, vicina *f*

neither: neither do I nemmeno io; **neither … nor …** né …, né …

nervous agitato

Netherlands Paesi Bassi *mpl*

never mai

new nuovo

news notizie *fpl*

newsagent giornalaio *m*

newspaper giornale *m*

news-stand edicola *f*

next prossimo

New Year capodanno *m*

nice bello; (person) simpatico

night notte *f* **35**, **39**

nightclub locale *m* notturno

nightdress camicia *f* da notte

no no; **no, thank you** no, grazie; **I'm in no hurry** non ho nessuna fretta

nobody nessuno

noise rumore *m*; **to make a noise** fare un rumore

noisy rumoroso

non-drinking water acqua *f* non potabile

none nessuno

non-smoking non fumatori

noon mezzogiorno *m*

north nord *m*; **in the north** a nord; **(to the) north of** a nord di

nose naso *m*

not non; **not yet** non ancora; **not any** nessuno; **not at all** per niente

note nota *f*

notebook taccuino *m*

nothing niente

novel romanzo *m*

November novembre *m*

now ora

nowadays al giorno d'oggi

nowhere da nessuna parte

number numero *m*

nurse infermiere *m*, infermiera *f*

---

obvious ovvio

ocean oceano *m*

o'clock: one o'clock l'una; **three o'clock** le tre

October ottobre *m*

of di

offer offrire

often spesso

oil olio *m*

ointment pomata *f*

OK va bene; **I'm OK** sto bene; **that's OK** non fa niente

old vecchio; **how old are you?** quanti anni hai?; **old people** gli anziani

old town centro *m* storico

on su; **it's on at …** lo danno al …
once una volta; **once a day/an hour** una volta al giorno/all'ora
one uno
only solo
open (adj) aperto
open (v) aprire
operate operare
operation: to have an operation subire un'operazione
opinion opinione f; **in my opinion** secondo me
opportunity opportunità f
opposite (n) contrario m
opposite (prep) di fronte a
optician ottico m
or o
orange arancia f
orchestra orchestra f
order (n) ordine m; **out of order** guasto
order (v) ordinare **44**
organic biologico
organize organizzare
other altro; **others** altri
otherwise altrimenti
our il nostro, la nostra, i nostri, le nostre
ours il nostro, la nostra, i nostri, le nostre
outside fuori
outward journey viaggio m di andata
oven forno m
over: over there lì
overdone troppo cotto
overweight: my luggage is overweight i miei bagagli superano il peso consentito

owe dovere **47**, **79**
own (adj) proprio; **my own car** la mia macchina
own (v) possedere
owner proprietario m, proprietaria f

P

pack: to pack one's suitcase preparare la valigia
package holiday viaggio m organizzato
packed pieno di gente
packet pacchetto m
painting dipinto m
pair paio m; **a pair of pyjamas** un pigiama; **a pair of shorts** un paio di pantaloni corti
palace palazzo m
pants mutande fpl
paper carta f; **paper napkin** tovagliolo m di carta; **paper tissue** fazzoletto m di carta
parcel pacchetto m
pardon? (mi) scusi?
parents genitori mpl
park (n) parco m
park (v) parcheggiare
parking space posto m (per la) macchina
part parte f; **to be a part of** far parte di
party festa f
pass (n) tesserino m
pass (v) passare
passenger passeggero m
passport passaporto m
past passato; **a quarter past ten** le dieci e un quarto

path sentiero m **72**
patient paziente mf
pay pagare **79**
pedestrian pedone m
pedestrianized street strada f pedonale
pee fare la pipì
peel sbucciare
pen penna f
pencil matita f
people la gente
percent per cento
perfect perfetto
perfume profumo m
perhaps forse
period mestruazioni fpl
person persona f
personal stereo Walkman® m
petrol benzina f
petrol station stazione f di servizio
phone (n) telefono m
phone (v) telefonare
phone box cabina f telefonica **95**
phone call telefonata f; **to make a phone call** fare una telefonata
phonecard scheda f telefonica **95**
phone number numero m di telefono
photo foto f; **to take a photo (of)** fare una foto (a) **85**; **to take someone's photo** fare una foto a qualcuno
picnic picnic m; **to have a picnic** fare un picnic
pie torta f
piece pezzo m; **a piece of** un pezzo di; **a piece of fruit** un frutto
piles emorroidi fpl

pill pillola f; **to be on the pill** prendere la pillola
pillow guanciale m
pillowcase federa f
PIN (number) codice m segreto
pink rosa
pity: it's a pity! peccato!
place posto m
plan programma m
plane aereo m
plant pianta f
plaster (cast) gesso m
plastic plastica f
plastic bag sacchetto m di plastica
plate piatto m
platform binario m **27**
play (n) spettacolo m teatrale
play (v) giocare
please (v) piacere a; **do as you please!** fai come ti pare!
please (adv) per favore
pleased contento; **pleased to meet you!** molto lieto!
pleasure piacere m
plug (electrical) spina f; (for sink etc) tappo m
plug in attaccare alla presa
plumber idraulico m
point punto m
police polizia f
policeman agente m (di polizia)
police station commissariato m **107**
policewoman agente f (di polizia)
pool piscina f **38**
poor povero
port porto m
portrait ritratto m
Portugal Portogallo m

Portuguese *(adj)* portoghese
Portuguese *(n) (language)* portoghese *m*; **the Portuguese** *(people)* i portoghesi
possible possibile
post *(n)* posta *f*
post *(v)* imbucare
postbox buca *f* delle lettere **90**
postcard cartolina *f*
postcode codice *m* postale
poste restante fermo posta *m*
poster poster *m*
postman postino *m*
post office ufficio *m* postale **90, 91**
pot *(for cooking)* pentola *f*; *(of yoghurt)* vasetto *m*
pound libbra *f*
powder polvere *f*
practical pratico
pram carrozzina *f*
prefer preferire
pregnant incinta **102**
prepare preparare
prescription ricetta *f*
present regalo *m*
press premere
pressure pressione *f*
previous precedente
price prezzo *m*
private privato
prize premio *m*
probably probabilmente
problem problema *m*
procession corteo *m*
product prodotto *m*
profession professione *f*
programme programma *m*
promise promettere
propose proporre

protect proteggere
proud (of) orgoglioso (di)
public pubblico
public holiday giorno *m* festivo
pull tirare
purple viola
purpose: on purpose apposta
purse borsellino *m*
push spingere
pushchair passeggino *m*
put mettere
put out spegnere
put up ospitare
put up with sopportare

---

quality qualità *f*; **of good/bad quality** di buona/cattiva qualità
quarter quarto *m*; **a quarter of an hour** un quarto d'ora; **a quarter to ten** le dieci meno un quarto
quay banchina *f*
question domanda *f*
queue *(n)* coda *f*
queue *(v)* fare la coda
quick veloce
quickly velocemente
quiet silenzioso
quite: quite a lot of parecchio; **quite a lot of time** parecchio tempo; **quite a lot of cars** parecchie macchine

---

R

racist razzista *mf*
racket racchetta *f*

radiator *(in room)* termosifone *m*; *(in car)* radiatore *m*

radio radio *f*

radio station stazione *f* radiofonica

rain pioggia *f*

rain: *(v)* **it's raining** piove

raincoat impermeabile *m*

random: at random a caso

rape stupro *m*

rare raro; *(meat)* al sangue

rarely raramente

rather piuttosto

raw crudo

razor rasoio *m*

razor blade lametta *f* (da barba)

reach raggiungere

read leggere

ready pronto

reasonable ragionevole

receipt *(from taxi)* ricevuta *f*; *(from shop)* scontrino *m* **79**

receive ricevere

reception reception *f*; **at reception** alla reception **37**

receptionist receptionist *mf*

recipe ricetta *f*

recognize riconoscere

recommend consigliare

red rosso

red light (semaforo) rosso *m*

red wine vino *m* rosso

reduce ridurre

reduction riduzione

refrigerator frigorifero *m*

refund *(n)* rimborso *m*; **to get a refund** ottenere un rimborso **82**

refund *(v)* rimborsare

refuse rifiutare

registered raccomandato

registration number numero *m* di targa

remember ricordare

remind ricordare

remove togliere

rent *(n)* affitto *m*

rent *(v)* affittare **38**

rental affitto *m*

reopen riaprire

repair riparare **30**; **to get something repaired** far riparare qualcosa

repeat ripetere **10**

reserve prenotare **35**, **43**

reserved prenotato

rest: *(n)* **the rest** il resto

rest *(v)* riposarsi

restaurant ristorante *m* **43**

return ritorno *m*

return ticket biglietto *m* di andata e ritorno

reverse-charge call chiamata *f* a carico del destinatario **95**

reverse gear retromarcia *f*

rheumatism reumatismi *mpl*

rib costola *f*

right *(n)* *(entitlement)* diritto *m*; *(right-hand side)* destra *f*; **to have the right to …** avere il diritto di …; **to the right (of)** a destra (di)

right *(adj)* *(correct)* giusto; *(right-hand)* destro

right: *(adv)* **right away** subito; **right beside** proprio accanto a

ring anello *m*

ripe maturo

rip-off furto *m*

risk rischio *m*

river fiume m
road strada f
road sign cartello m stradale
rock roccia f
rollerblades Rollerblade® mpl
room camera f **35**, **36**
rosé wine vino m rosato
round rotondo
roundabout rotatoria f
rubbish spazzatura f; **to take the rubbish out** portare fuori la spazzatura
rucksack zaino m
rug tappeto m
ruins rovine fpl; **in ruins** in rovina
run out: to have run out of petrol essere rimasto senza benzina **30**

S

sad triste
safe sicuro
safety sicurezza f
safety belt cintura f di sicurezza
sail navigare
sailing vela f; **to go sailing** fare vela
sale: for sale in vendita
sales saldi mpl; **in the sales** in saldo
salt sale m
salted salato
salty salato
same stesso; **the same** lo stesso **47**
sand sabbia f
sandals sandali mpl
sanitary towel assorbente m (igienico)

Saturday sabato m
saucepan tegame m
save risparmiare
say dire; **how do you say… ?** come si dice …?
scared: to be scared (of) aver paura (di)
scenery paesaggio m
scissors forbici fpl
scoop: one/two scoop(s) (of ice cream) una pallina/due palline
scooter scooter m
Scot scozzese mf
scotch (whisky) scotch m
Scotland Scozia f
Scottish scozzese
scuba diving immersione f
sea mare m
seafood frutti mpl di mare
seasick: to be seasick avere il mal di mare
seaside: at the seaside al mare
seaside resort località f balneare
season stagione f
seat posto m (a sedere) **23**
sea view vista f sul mare
seaweed alga f marina
second secondo
second class seconda classe f
secondary school scuola f secondaria
second-hand di seconda mano
secure sicuro
security sicurezza f
see vedere; **see you later!** a dopo!; **see you soon!** a presto!; **see you tomorrow!** a domani!
seem sembrare; **it seems that …** sembra che …

seldom di rado
sell vendere **78**
Sellotape® Scotch® *m*
send spedire
sender mittente *m*
sense senso *m*
sensitive sensibile
sentence frase *f*
separate separato
separately separatamente
September settembre *m*
serious serio
service servicio *m* **47**
service station stazione *f* di servizio **29**
several parecchi
sex sesso *m*
shade ombra *f*; **in the shade** all'ombra
shame vergogna *f*
shampoo shampoo *m*
shape forma *f*
share dividere
shave farsi la barba
shaving cream crema *f* da barba
shaving foam schiuma *f* da barba
she lei
sheet *(for bed)* lenzuolo *m*; *(of paper)* foglio *m*
shellfish frutti *mpl* di mare
shirt camicia *f*
shock shock *m*
shocking scioccante
shoes scarpe *fpl*
shop negozio *m*
shop assistant commesso *m*, commessa *f*
shopkeeper negoziante *mf*

shopping acquisti *mpl*; **to do some shopping** fare acquisti; **to do the shopping** fare la spesa
shopping centre centro *m* commerciale
short corto; **I'm two ... short** mi mancano due ...
short cut scorciatoia *f*
shorts calzoncini *mpl*
short-sleeved a maniche corte
shoulder spalla *f*
show *(n)* spettacolo *m*
show *(v)* mostrare
shower doccia *f*; **to take a shower** fare la doccia
shower gel gel *m* da doccia
shut chiudere
shutter persiana *f*
shuttle navetta *f*
sick: to feel sick avere la nausea
side lato *m*
sign *(n)* cartello *m*
sign *(v)* firmare
signal segnale *m*
silent silenzioso
silver argento *m*
silver-plated placcato (d')argento
since da
sing cantare
singer cantante *mf*
single single
single (ticket) biglietto *m* di sola andata
sister sorella *f*
sit down sedersi
size taglia *f*
ski *(n)* sci *m*
ski *(v)* sciare

skiing sci m; **to go skiing** andare a sciare
ski lift ski-lift m
ski pole racchetta f da sci
ski resort località f sciistica
skin pelle f
skirt gonna f
sky cielo m
skyscraper grattacielo m
sleep (n) sonno m
sleep (v) dormire; **to sleep with** andare a letto con
sleeping bag sacco m a pelo
sleeping pill sonnifero m
sleepy: to be sleepy avere sonno
sleeve manica f
slice fetta f
sliced a fette
slide diapositiva f
slow lento
slowly lentamente
small piccolo
smell (n) odore m
smell (v) sentire odore di; **to smell good/bad** avere un buon/cattivo odore
smile (n) sorriso m
smile (v) sorridere
smoke (v) fumare
smoke (n) fumo m
smoker fumatore m, fumatrice f
snack: to have a snack fare uno spuntino
snow (n) neve f
snow (v) nevicare
so così; **so that** in modo che
soap sapone m
soccer calcio m
socks calze fpl

some un po' di; **some bread** un po' di pane; **some people** alcune persone
somebody qualcuno
someone qualcuno
something qualcosa; **something else** qualcos'altro
sometimes a volte
somewhere da qualche parte; **somewhere else** da qualche altra parte
son figlio m
song canzone f
soon presto
sore: to have a sore throat avere mal di gola; **to have a sore head** avere male alla testa
sorry: I'm sorry mi dispiace; **sorry!** scusi!
south sud m; **in the south** a sud; **(to the) south of** a sud di
souvenir souvenir m
Spain Spagna f
Spanish (adj) spagnolo
Spanish (n) (language) spagnolo m; **the Spanish** (people) gli spagnoli
spare part (pezzo m di) ricambio m
spare tyre gomma f di scorta
spare wheel ruota f di scorta
spark plug candela f
speak parlare **8**, **10**, **96**, **107**
special speciale; **today's special** il piatto del giorno **45**
speciality specialità f
speed velocità f; **at full speed** a tutta velocità
spell scrivere; **how do you spell it?** come si scrive?
spend spendere

spice spezia *f*

spicy piccante

spider ragno *m*

splinter scheggia *f*

split up separarsi

spoil rovinare

sponge spugna *f*

spoon cucchiaio *m*

sport sport *m*

sports ground terreno *m* sportivo

sporty sportivo

spot brufolo *f*

sprain: to sprain one's ankle
slogarsi la caviglia

spring primavera *f*

square piazza *f*

stadium stadio *m*

stain macchia *f*

stained-glass windows vetrate
fpl

stairs scale *fpl*

stamp francobollo *m* **91**

start cominciare

state stato *m*

statement affermazione *f*

station stazione *f*

stay *(n)* soggiorno *m*

stay *(v)* rimanere; **to stay in**
touch rimanere in contatto

steal rubare **107**

step gradino *m*

sticking plaster cerotto *m*
adesivo

still ancora

still water acqua *f* naturale

sting *(n)* puntura *f*

sting *(v)* pungere; **to get stung**
(by) essere punto (da)

stock: out of stock esaurito

stomach stomaco *m*

stomachache mal *m* di pancia

stone pietra *f*

stop *(n)* fermata *f* **28**

stop *(v)* fermarsi; **to stop doing**
something smettere di fare
qualcosa

stopcock rubinetto *m* (di arresto)

storey piano *m*

storm temporale *m*

straight ahead, straight on
sempre dritto

strange strano

street via *f*

strong forte

stuck bloccato

student studente *m*, studentessa
f **15**, **23**

studies studi *mpl*

study studiare; **to study biology**
studiare biologia

style stile *m*

subtitled sottotitolato

suburb quartiere *m* periferico

suffer (from) soffrire (di)

suggest suggerire

suit: does that suit you? ti va bene?

suitcase valigia *f* **25**

summer estate *f*

summit cima *f*

sun sole *m*; **in the sun** al sole

sunbathe prendere il sole

sunburnt: to get sunburnt
scottarsi al sole

sun cream crema *f* solare

Sunday domenica *f*

sunglasses occhiali *mpl* da sole

sunhat cappello *m* da sole

sunrise alba *f*

sunset tramonto *m*

sunstroke insolazione *f*; **to get sunstroke** prendere un'insolazione

supermarket supermercato *m* **39**, **77**

supplement supplemento *m*

sure sicuro

surf fare surf

surfboard surf *m*

surfing surf *m*; **to go surfing** fare surf

surgical spirit alcol *m* denaturato

surname cognome *m*

surprise *(n)* sorpresa *f*

surprise *(v)* sorprendere

sweat *(n)* sudore *m*

sweat *(v)* sudare

sweater golf *m*

sweet *(n)* caramella *f*

sweet *(adj)* dolce

swim: (n) to go for a swim fare una nuotata

swim *(v)* nuotare

swimming nuoto *m*

swimming pool piscina *f* **73**

swimming trunks calzoncini *mpl* da bagno

swimsuit costume *m* intero

switch off spegnere

switch on accendere

switchboard operator centralinista *mf*

swollen gonfio

synagogue sinagoga *f*

syrup sciroppo *m*

T

table tavolo *m* **43**, **44**

tablespoon cucchiaio *m*

tablet compressa *f*

take prendere; **it takes 2 hours** ci vogliono due ore

take off *(plane)* decollare

takeaway piatto *m* da asporto

talk parlare

tall alto

tampon assorbente *m* interno

tan *(v)* abbronzarsi

tan *(n)* abbronzatura *f*

tanned abbronzato

tap rubinetto *m*

taste *(n)* gusto *m*

taste *(v)* assaggiare

tax tassa *f*

tax-free esentasse

taxi taxi *m* **30**

taxi driver tassista *mf*

team squadra *f*

teaspoon cucchiaino *m*

teenager adolescente *mf*

telephone *(n)* telefono *m*

telephone *(v)* telefonare

television televisione *f*

tell dire

temperature temperatura *f* **102**; **to take one's temperature** misurarsi la febbre

temple tempia *f*

temporary temporaneo

tennis tennis *m*

tennis court campo *m* da tennis

tennis shoe scarpa *f* da tennis

tent tenda *f*

tent peg picchetto m
terminal terminale m
terrace terrazza f
terrible terribile
thank ringraziare; **thank you** grazie; **thank you very much** grazie mille
thanks grazie; **thanks to** grazie a
that quello; **that one** quello (lì)
the il, la, i, le
theatre teatro m
theft furto m
their il loro, la loro, i loro, le loro
theirs il loro, la loro, i loro, le loro
them *(direct object)* li mpl, le fpl; *(indirect object)* (a) loro, gli
theme park parco m a tema
then allora; (afterwards) poi
there lì; **there is** c'è; **there are** ci sono
therefore pertanto
thermometer termometro m
Thermos® flask thermos m
these questi; **these ones** questi (qui)
they loro; **they say that …** si dice che …
thief ladro m, ladra f
thigh coscia f
thin magro
thing cosa f
think pensare
think about riflettere su
thirst sete f
thirsty: to be thirsty avere sete
this questo; **this one** questo (qui); **this evening** stasera; **this is …** ti presento …
those quelli; **those ones** quelli (lì)

throat gola f
throw tirare
throw out buttare fuori
Thursday giovedì m
ticket biglietto m **23**, **60**, **61**
ticket office biglietteria f
tidy ordinato
tie cravatta f
tight stretto
tights collant m
time tempo m **114**; *(occasion)* volta f; **what time is it?** che ore sono?; **from time to time** di tanto in tanto; **on time** in orario; **three/four times** tre/quattro volte
time difference differenza f di fuso orario
timetable orario m **23**
tinfoil stagnola f
tip mancia f
tired stanco
tobacco tabacco m
tobacconist's tabaccheria f
today oggi
together insieme
toilet toilette f **8**, **43**
toilet bag borsa f da toilette
toilet paper carta f igienica
toiletries articoli mpl da toilette
toll pedaggio m
tomorrow domani; **tomorrow evening** domani sera; **tomorrow morning** domattina
tongue lingua f
tonight *(evening)* stasera; *(night)* stanotte
too *(also)* anche; (excessively) troppo; **too bad** peccato; **too many** troppi; **too much** troppo

tooth dente *m*
toothbrush spazzolino *m* da denti
toothpaste dentifricio *m*
top cima *f*; **at the top** in cima
torch torcia *f* elettrica
touch toccare
tourist turista *mf*
tourist office ufficio *m* turistico **65**
tourist trap trappola *f* per turisti
towards verso
towel asciugamano *m*
town città *f*
town centre centro *m*
town hall municipio *m*
toy giocattolo *m*
traditional tradizionale
traffic traffico *m*
traffic jam ingorgo *m* stradale
train treno *m* **28**; **the train to Florence** il treno per Firenze
train station stazione *f* ferroviaria
tram tram *m*
transfer *(of money)* bonifico *m*
translate tradurre
travel agency agenzia *f* di viaggi
travel viaggiare
traveller's cheque traveller's cheque *m*
trip viaggio *m*; **have a good trip!** buon viaggio!
trolley carrello *m*
trouble: to have trouble doing something avere difficoltà a fare qualcosa
trousers pantaloni *mpl*
true vero
try provare; **to try to do something** provare a fare qualcosa

try on provare **81**
Tuesday martedì *m*
tube metro *f*
tube station stazione *f* della metro
turn: *(n)* **it's your turn** tocca a te
turn *(v)* girare
twice due volte
type *(n)* tipo *m*
type *(v)* battere (al computer)
typical tipico
tyre pneumatico *m*

umbrella ombrello *m*
uncle zio *m*
uncomfortable scomodo
under sotto
underground metropolitana *f* **27**
underground line linea *f* della metropolitana
underground station stazione *f* della metropolitana
underneath sotto
understand capire **10**
underwear biancheria *f* intima
United Kingdom Regno Unito *m*
United States Stati Uniti *mpl*
unleaded petrol benzina *f* senza piombo
until fino a
upset contrariato
upstairs di sopra
urgent urgente
us *(direct object)* ci; *(indirect object)* ci, a noi

use usare; **to be used for** servire a; **I'm used to it** ci sono abituato
useful utile
useless inutile
usually di solito
U-turn inversione *f* a U

vaccinated (against) vaccinato (contro)
valid (for) valido (per)
valley valle *f*
VAT IVA *f*
vegetarian vegetariano
very molto
view vista *f*
villa villa *f*
village paese *m*
visa visto *m*
visit *(n)* visita *f*
visit *(v)* visitare
volleyball pallavolo *f*
vomit vomitare

waist vita *f*
wait aspettare; **to wait for** aspettare
waiter cameriere *m*
waitress cameriera *f*
wake up svegliarsi
Wales Galles *m*
walk: *(n)* **to go for a walk** andare a fare una passeggiata
walk *(v)* camminare
walking: to go walking fare un'escursione (a piedi)

walking boots scarponi *mpl* da montagna
Walkman® Walkman® *m*
wallet portafoglio *m*
want volere; **to want to do something** voler fare qualcosa
warm caldo
warn avvertire
wash: to have a wash lavarsi
wash *(v)* lavare; **to wash one's hair** lavarsi i capelli
washbasin lavandino *m*
washing: to do the washing lavare i panni
washing machine lavatrice *f*
washing powder detersivo *m* in polvere
washing-up liquid detersivo *m* liquido (per i piatti)
wasp vespa *f*
waste sprecare
watch *(n)* orologio *m*
watch *(v)* guardare; **watch out!** attenzione!
water acqua *f* **45**
water heater scaldabagno *m*
waterproof impermeabile
waterskiing sci *m* acquatico
wave onda *f*
way *(manner)* modo *m*; *(direction)* direzione *f*
way in entrata *f*
way out uscita *f*
we noi
weak debole
wear indossare
weather tempo *m* **20**, **21**; **the weather's bad** è brutto tempo

weather forecast previsioni *fpl* del tempo **20**
website sito *m* web
Wednesday mercoledì *m*
week settimana *f*
weekend fine settimana *m*
welcome benvenuto; **welcome!** benvenuto!; **you're welcome** non c'è di che
well bene; **I'm very well** sto benissimo; **well done** *(meat)* ben cotto
well-known noto
Welsh *(adj)* gallese
Welsh *(n)* *(language)* gallese *m*; **the Welsh** *(people)* i gallesi
west ovest *m*; **in the west** a ovest; **(to the) west of** a ovest di
wet bagnato
wetsuit muta *f*
what cosa; **what do you want?** cosa vuoi?
wheel ruota *f*
wheelchair sedia *f* a rotelle
when quando
where dove; **where is/are …?** dov'è/dove sono …?; **where are you from?** da dove vieni?; **where are you going?** dove vai?
which quale
while mentre
white bianco
white wine vino *m* bianco
who chi; **who's calling?** chi parla?
whole intero; **the whole cake** tutta la torta

whose il cui, la cui, i cui, le cui; **whose jacket is this?** di chi è questa giacca?
why perché
wide largo
wife moglie *f*
wild selvaggio
wind vento *m*
window finestra *f*; **in the window** in vetrina **82**
windscreen parabrezza *m*
windsurfing windsurf *m*
wine vino *m* **45**, **46**
winter inverno *m*
with con
withdraw *(money)* prelevare
without senza
woman donna *f*
wonderful meraviglioso
wood *(material)* legno *m*; *(forest)* bosco *m*
wool lana *f*
work *(n)* lavoro *m*; **work of art** opera *f* d'arte
work *(v)* lavorare
world mondo *m*
worse *(adj)* peggiore; **to get worse** peggiorare; **it's worse (than)** è peggiore (di)
worse *(adv)* peggio
worth: to be worth valere; **it's worth it** ne vale la pena
wound ferita *f*
wrist polso *m*
write scrivere **10**, **79**
wrong sbagliato; **you're wrong** ti sbagli

XYZ

X-ray radiografia *f*

year anno *m*
yellow giallo
yes sì
yesterday ieri; **yesterday evening** ieri sera
you *(sing)* *(subject)* tu; *(direct object)* ti; *(indirect object)* ti, a te; *(pl)* *(subject)* voi; *(direct object)* vi; *(indirect object)* vi, a voi
young giovane
your *(sing)* il tuo, la tua, i tuoi, le tue; *(pl)* il vostro, la vostra, i vostri, le vostre

yours *(sing)* il tuo, la tua, i tuoi, le tue; *(pl)* il vostro, la vostra, i vostri, le vostre
youth hostel ostello *m* della gioventù

zero zero *m*
zip cerniera *f*
zoo zoo *m*
zoom (lens) zoom *m*

DICTIONARY

ITALIAN-ENGLISH

A

a at; **a 10 miglia** 10 miles away
abbastanza enough
abbazia *f* abbey
abbigliamento *m* clothes
abbronzarsi to tan
abbronzato tanned
abbronzatura *f* tan
abiti *mpl* clothes
abituato: ci sono abituato I'm used to it
accanto a beside
accendere to light *(cigarette)*; to switch on *(light)*; **ha da accendere?** do you have a light?
accendino *m* lighter
accesso *m* access
accettare to accept
accompagnare to go with
acqua *f* water
acqua *f* **minerale** mineral water
acqua *f* **naturale** still water
acqua *f* **non potabile** non-drinking water
acqua *f* **potabile** drinking water
acquisti *mpl* shopping; **fare acquisti** to do some shopping
adattatore *m* adaptor
addormentarsi to fall asleep
adolescente *mf* teenager
aereo *m* plane

aeroplano *m* aeroplane
aeroporto *m* airport
affermazione *f* statement
affittare to rent
affitto *m* rent, rental
affollato busy *(place)*
agente *m* **(di polizia)** policeman
agente *f* **(di polizia)** policewoman
agenzia *f* **di viaggi** travel agency
aggredire to attack
agitato nervous
agosto *m* August
aiutare to help
aiuto *m* help; **chiamare aiuto** to call for help; **aiuto!** help!
alba *f* sunrise
albergo *m* hotel
alcol *m* alcohol
alcol *m* **denaturato** surgical spirit
alcuni some; **alcune persone** some people
alga *f* **marina** seaweed
allergico allergic
allora then
almeno at least
alpinismo *m* climbing
alta marea *f* high tide
alto high, tall
altrimenti otherwise
altro other; **un altro** *m*, **un'altra** *f* another; **altri** others

altroieri: l'altroieri the day before yesterday

alzarsi to get up

ambasciata *f* embassy

ambulanza *f* ambulance

americano American *(adj)*

americano *m*, **americana** *f* American *(n)*

amico *m*, **amica** *f* friend

ammalarsi to fall ill

anatra *f* duck

anche also, too

ancora still; **non ancora** not yet

andare to go; **andiamo** let's go; **andare via** to go away; **andare a Roma/in Italia** to go to Rome/to Italy; **andiamo a casa domani** we're going home tomorrow

anello *m* ring

anestesia *f* anaesthetic

animale *m* animal

annegare to drown

anniversario *m* anniversary

anno *m* year; **quanti anni hai?** how old are you?; **ho ventidue anni** I'm 22 (years old)

annullare to cancel

antibiotici *mpl* antibiotics

anticipo *m*: **in anticipo** in advance

anziano old; **gli anziani** old people

ape *f* bee

aperto open *(adj)*

apertura *f* **notturna** late-night opening

appartamento *m* flat

appena *(adv)* just; **sono appena arrivato** I've just arrived

appena *(conj)*: **(non) appena** as soon as

appendicite *f* appendicitis

appetito *m*: **buon appetito!** enjoy your meal!

apposta on purpose

appuntamento *m* appointment; **prendere (un) appuntamento** to make an appointment; **avere un appuntamento (con)** to have an appointment (with)

apribottiglie *m* bottle opener

aprile *m* April

aprire to open

apriscatole *m* tin opener, can opener

arancia *f* orange

argento *m* silver

aria *f* air; **avere l'aria stanca** to look tired

aria *f* **condizionata** air conditioning

arrivare to arrive

arrivederci! goodbye!, bye!

arrivo *m* arrival

arte *f* art

articoli *mpl* **da toilette** toiletries

articolo *m* item

artista *mf* artist

ascensore *m* lift *(elevator)*

asciugamano *m* towel

asciugamano *m* **da bagno** bath towel

asciugare to dry

asciutto dry

ascoltare to listen; **ascoltare qualcuno/qualcosa** to listen to someone/something

asma *f* asthma

aspettare to wait; **aspettare qualcuno/qualcosa** to wait for someone/something
aspirina *f* aspirin
assaggiare to taste
assegno *m* cheque
assicurazione *f* insurance
assicurazione *f* **kasko** comprehensive insurance
assorbente m **(igienico)** sanitary towel
assorbente *m* **interno** tampon
attaccapanni *m* coathanger
attaccare: attaccare alla presa to plug in
attenzione! watch out!
attraversare to cross
attraverso across
attrezzatura *f* equipment
attualmente at the moment
autobus *m* bus
autostop *m* hitchhiking; **fare l'autostop** to hitchhike
autostrada *f* motorway
autunno *m* autumn
avanti: in avanti forward *(adj)*
avere to have
avvertire to warn
avvocato *m* lawyer

B

bagagli *mpl* luggage, baggage; **un bagaglio** a piece of luggage
bagaglio *m* **a mano** hand luggage
bagnato wet
bagno *m* bathroom, bath; **fare il bagno** to have a bath

bagno *m* **degli uomini** gents' (toilet)
bagno *m* **delle donne** ladies' (toilet)
balcone *m* balcony
ballare to dance
ballo *m* dance
bambino *m*, **bambina** *f* child
bambino (piccolo) *m*, **bambina (piccola)** *f* baby
banca *f* bank
banchina *f* quay
bancomat® *m* cashpoint, debit card
banconota *f* banknote
bar *m* bar
barba *f* beard; **farsi la barba** to shave
barca *f* boat
bassa marea *f* low tide
basso low
basta that's enough
battere (al computer) to type
batteria *f* battery
belga Belgian *(adj)*
belga *mf* Belgian *(n)*
Belgio *m* Belgium
bello beautiful, nice
benda *f* bandage
bene well; **sto bene** I'm fine, I'm OK; **sto benissimo** I'm very well; **va bene** OK, it's fine; **ti va bene?** does that suit you?; **ben cotto** well done *(meat)*
benvenuto welcome; **benvenuto!** welcome!
benzina *f* petrol
bere to drink; **bere qualcosa** to have a drink; **andare a bere qualcosa** to go for a drink

bernoccolo m bump
bevanda f drink
bevanda f **calda** hot drink
biancheria f **intima** underwear
bianco white
biberon m baby's bottle
biblioteca f library
bicchiere m glass; **un bicchiere d'acqua/di vino** a glass of water/ of wine
bici f bike
bicicletta f bicycle
bidone m **(della spazzatura)** bin
biglietteria f ticket office
biglietto m ticket
biglietto m **di andata e ritorno** return ticket
biglietto m **di sola andata** single (ticket)
binario m platform
binocolo m binoculars
biologico organic
birra f beer
birra f **alla spina** draught beer
birra f **piccola** half-pint
bisogno m: **aver bisogno di** to need
bloccato stuck
blu blue
boa f buoy
bocca f mouth
bombola f **del gas** gas cylinder
bonifico m transfer (of money)
borsa f bag
borsa f **da toilette** toilet bag
borsellino m purse
borsetta f handbag
bosco m wood (forest)
bottiglia f bottle

braccio m arm
bricco m jug (for milk, coffee)
bronchite f bronchitis
bruciare to burn; **bruciarsi** to burn oneself
bruciatura f burn
brufolo f spot (pimple)
buca f **delle lettere** letterbox, postbox
buonanotte goodnight
buonasera good evening
buongiorno good morning, good afternoon
buono good
busta f envelope
buttare to throw; **buttare fuori** to throw out

C

cabina f **di prova** changing room (in shop)
cabina f **telefonica** phone box
cadere to fall
caffè m coffee, café
caffè m **(espresso)** espresso, expresso
caffè m **solubile** instant coffee
calcio m football, soccer
caldo warm, hot; **fa caldo** it's warm, it's hot (weather)
calore m heat
calze fpl socks
calzoncini mpl shorts
calzoncini mpl **da bagno** swimming trunks
cambiare to change
cambio m change; exchange (currency)

cameriera f waitress
cameriere m waiter
camerino m fitting room
camicia f shirt
camicia f **da notte** nightdress
camino m chimney
camion m lorry
camminare to walk
campagna f countryside
campeggiatore m, **campeggiatrice** f camper (person)
campeggio m campsite, camping; **andare in campeggio** to go camping
camper m camper (van)
campo m **da golf** golf course
campo m **da tennis** tennis court
canale m channel
cancello m gate
candela f candle, spark plug
cantante mf singer
cantare to sing
canzone f song
capelli mpl hair
capire to understand
capodanno m New Year
cappella f chapel
cappello m hat
cappello m **da sole** sunhat
caraffa f jug (for wine, water)
caramella f sweet
caricare to charge (battery, mobile)
carnet m **di biglietti** book of tickets
caro dear, expensive
carrello m trolley
carrozzina f pram

carta f paper
carta f **da regalo** gift wrap
carta f **di credito** credit card
carta f **d'identità** identity card
carta f **igienica** toilet paper
cartello m sign
cartello m **stradale** road sign
cartina f map
cartine fpl **(per sigarette)** cigarette paper
cartolina f postcard
casa f house, home; **a casa** at home; **andare a casa** to go home
casco m helmet
caso m case; **in caso di ...** in case of ...; **a caso** at random
casomai just in case
cassa f checkout
castello m castle
cattedrale f cathedral
cattivo bad
causa f: **a causa di** because of
cauzione f deposit
cavallo m horse
cavarsela to manage
cavatappi m corkscrew
caviglia f ankle
cd m CD
cellulare m mobile (phone)
cena f dinner
cenare to have dinner
centimetro m centimetre
cento: per cento percent
centralinista mf switchboard operator
centro m centre, town centre
centro m **commerciale** shopping centre

centro *m* **storico** old town
cercare to look for
cerniera *f* zip
cerotto *m* Elastoplast®
cerotto *m* **adesivo** sticking
   plaster
certo of course
check-in *m* check-in; **fare il
   check-in** to check in
chi who; **chi parla?** who's calling?;
   di chi è questa giacca? whose
   jacket is this?
chiamare to call; **chiamarsi** to be
   called; **mi chiamo …** my name
   is …
chiamata *f* call
chiamata *f* **a carico del
   destinatario** reverse-charge call
chiaro light; **verde chiaro** light
   green
chiave *f* key
chiedere to ask
chiesa *f* church
chiodo *m* nail *(metal)*
chiudere to close, to shut;
   chiudere a chiave to lock
chiunque anybody, anyone
chiuso closed, shut
ci *(pron)* us, to us, ourselves, to
   ourselves
ci *(adv)* there; **c'è** there is; **ci sono**
   there are
cibo *m* food
cieco blind *(adj)*
cielo *m* sky
cima *f* top, summit; **in cima** at
   the top
cimitero *m* cemetery
cincin! cheers!

cinema *m* cinema
cintura *f* **di sicurezza** safety belt
cioccolata *f* **calda** hot chocolate
cioccolato *m* chocolate
circa about
circo *m* circus
città *f* town, city
classe *f* **economica** economy
   class
clima *m* climate
Coca-Cola® *f* Coke®
coda *f* queue; **fare la coda** to
   queue
codice *m* **apriporta** door code
codice *m* **postale** postcode
codice *m* **segreto** PIN (number)
cognome *m* surname
coincidenza *f* connection
   (transport)
colazione *f* breakfast; **fare
   colazione** to have breakfast
collant *m* tights
collezione *f* collection
collina *f* hill
collo *m* neck
colore *m* colour
coltello *m* knife
**combinare: combinare di
   incontrarsi** to arrange to meet
come how, as, like; **come va?**
   how are you?; **(così) come** as
   well as
cominciare to start
commesso *m*, **commessa** *f* shop
   assistant
commissariato *m* police station
comodo comfortable
compagnia *f* **aerea** airline
compilare to fill in, to fill out

compleanno m birthday
comprare to buy
compreso included
compressa f tablet
computer m computer
comunque anyway, all the same
con with
concerto m concert
condimento m dressing
confermare to confirm
congelatore m freezer
consigli mpl advice; **chiedere consiglio a qualcuno** to ask someone's advice
consigliare to advise, to recommend
consolato m consulate
contagioso contagious
contanti mpl cash; **pagare in contanti** to pay cash
contare to count
contatore m meter
contatore m **della luce** electricity meter
contattare to contact
contatto m contact
contento pleased
continuare: continuare a fare qualcosa to keep doing something
conto m bill
contraccettivo m contraceptive
contrariato upset
contrario m opposite
contro against
coperta f blanket, cover
copertina f cover (of book, magazine)
coprire to cover

corpo m body
corteo m procession
corto short
cosa f thing
cosa what; **cosa vuoi?** what do you want?
coscia f thigh
così so
costa f coast
costare to cost
costo m cost, charge
costola f rib
costruire to build
costume m **intero** swimsuit
cotone m cotton
cotto cooked; **troppo cotto** overdone; **non troppo cotto** medium (meat)
cotton fioc® m cotton bud
cravatta f tie
credere to believe
crema f **da barba** shaving cream
crema f **idratante** moisturizer
crema f **solare** sun cream
crescere to grow
croce f cross
crociera f cruise
crudo raw
cubetto m **di ghiaccio** ice cube
cucchiaino m teaspoon
cucchiaio m spoon, tablespoon
cucina f kitchen, cooking
cucinare to cook, to do the cooking
cui: il cui, la cui, i cui, le cui whose
cuocere (in forno) to bake
cuore m heart

D

da from, by, since; **da … a …** from … to …

danneggiato damaged

dappertutto everywhere

dare to give; **lo danno al …** it's on at … *(film)*

data *f* date

data *f* **di nascita** date of birth

data *f* **di scadenza** expiry date

davanti *m* front; **davanti a** in front of

debole weak

decollare to take off *(plane)*

dehors *m* terrace

dente *m* tooth

dentifricio *m* toothpaste

dentista *mf* dentist

dentro inside

deodorante *m* deodorant

dépliant *m* brochure

deposito *m* **bagagli** left-luggage (office)

destra *f* right; **a destra (di)** to the right (of)

destro right *(adj)*

detersivo *m* **in polvere** washing powder

detersivo *m* **liquido (per i piatti)** washing-up liquid

di of

diabete *m* diabetes

diapositiva *f* slide

diarrea *f* diarrhoea; **avere la diarrea** to have diarrhoea

dicembre *m* December

dichiarare to declare

diesel *m* diesel

dieta *f* diet; **essere a dieta** to be on a diet

dietro behind

difetto *m* flaw

differenza *f* **di fuso orario** time difference

difficile difficult

difficoltà *f* difficulty; **avere difficoltà a fare qualcosa** to have trouble doing something

dipendere: dipende (da) that depends (on)

dipinto *m* painting

dire to say, to tell; **come si dice …?** how do you say… ?; **si dice che …** they say that …

diretto direct

direttore *m*, **direttrice** *f* manager

direzione *f* direction, way

diritto *m* right; **avere il diritto di …** to have the right to …

disabile disabled

disastro *m* disaster

discoteca *f* club

disinfettare to disinfect

dispiacere: mi dispiace I'm sorry

disponibile available

disturbare to disturb; **non disturbare** do not disturb

dito *m* finger

diverso (da) different (from)

divertirsi to enjoy oneself

dividere to share

doccia *f* shower; **fare la doccia** to take a shower

documenti *mpl* **d'identità** identity papers

dogana *f* customs

dolce sweet *(adj)*
dolce *m* dessert
domanda *f* question; **fare una domanda** to ask a question
domani tomorrow; **domani sera** tomorrow evening; **a domani!** see you tomorrow!
domattina tomorrow morning
domenica *f* Sunday
donna *f* woman
dopo after; **a dopo!** see you later!
dopodomani the day after tomorrow
doposole *m* after-sun (cream)
dormire to sleep
dove where; **dov'è/dove sono …?** where is/are …?; **da dove vieni?** where are you from?; **dove vai?** where are you going?
dovere to have to, must, to owe; **devo andare** I have to go, I must go; **devono essere le cinque** it must be 5 o'clock
droga *f* drugs
durante during; **durante la settimana** during the week
durare to last
duro hard

E

e and
eccedenza *f* excess
eccezionale exceptional
ecco here is/are
economico cheap
edicola *f* news-stand
edificio *m* building
elenco *m* **telefonico** directory

elettricità *f* electricity
elettrico electric
e-mail *f* e-mail
emergenza *f* emergency; **in caso di emergenza** in an emergency
emorroidi *fpl* piles
entrambi both
entrare to come in, to go in
entrata *f* way in
epilettico epileptic
erba *f* grass
errore *m* mistake; **fare un errore** to make a mistake
esaurito out of stock
escursione *f*: **fare un'escursione (a piedi)** to go walking; **fare delle escursioni** to go hiking; **fare delle escursioni in bassa montagna** to go hill-walking
esentasse tax-free
espresso express *(adj)*
essere to be; **sono inglese** I'm English
est east; **a est** in the east; **a est di** (to the) east of
estate *f* summer
estero *m*: **all'estero** abroad
età *f* age
euro *m* euro
eurocheque *m* Eurocheque
Europa *f* Europe
europeo European
ex former
extra extra

F

faccia *f* face

facile easy
fame *f* hunger; **avere fame** to be hungry
famiglia *f* family
fare to do, to make
farmacia *f* chemist's
farmacia *f* **di turno** duty chemist's
faro *m* headlight, lighthouse
fast food *m* fast-food restaurant
fatto *m* fact
fatto a mano hand-made
favore *m* favour; **fare un favore a qualcuno** to do someone a favour; **per favore** please
fax *m* fax
fazzoletto *m* handkerchief
fazzoletto *m* **di carta** paper tissue
febbraio *m* February
febbre *f* fever; **avere la febbre** to have a fever; **misurarsi la febbre** to take one's temperature
federa *f* pillowcase
fegato *m* liver
felice happy
ferita *f* wound
ferito injured
fermarsi to stop
fermata *f* stop
fermata *f* **dell'autobus** bus stop
fermo posta *m* poste restante
ferro *m* iron *(metal)*
ferro *m* **da stiro** iron *(for ironing)*
festa *f* party
festa *f* **nazionale** national holiday
festival *m* festival
fetta *f* slice; **a fette** sliced
fiammifero *m* match *(for cigarette)*

fianco *m* hip
fidanzata *f* fiancée
fidanzato *m* fiancé
fiducia *f* **in se stesso** self-confidence
fiera *f* fair
figlia *f* daughter
figlio *m* son
film *m* film, movie
fine *f* end; **alla fine** finally; **alla fine di** at the end of
fine settimana *m* weekend
finestra *f* window
finire to finish
fino a until
firmare to sign
fiume *m* river
flash *m* flash *(on camera)*
foglio *m* sheet *(of paper)*
fon *m* hairdrier
fondo *m* bottom; **in fondo** at the bottom; **in fondo a** at the bottom of, at the back of; **in fondo alla strada** at the end of the street
forbici *fpl* scissors
forchetta *f* fork
foresta *f* forest
forma *f* shape
formica *f* ant
fornello *m* **da campeggio** camping stove
forno *m* oven
forno *m* **a microonde** microwave
forse perhaps, maybe
forte strong, loud
fortuna *f* luck
fortunato lucky
foto *f* photo; **fare una foto (a)** to take a photo (of); **fare una foto**

a qualcuno to take someone's photo
fragile fragile
francese French *(adj)*
francese *m* French *(language)*;
 i francesi the French *(people)*
Francia *f* France
francobollo *m* stamp
frase *f* sentence
fratello *m* brother
frattura *f* fracture
freccia *f* **(di direzione)** indicator
 (of car)
freddo cold, chilly; **fa freddo** it's
 cold *(weather)*; **ho freddo** I'm
 cold
frenare to brake
freno *m* brake
freno *m* **a mano** handbrake
fresco cool
fretta *f*: **avere fretta** to be in
 a hurry
friggere to fry
frigorifero *m* fridge, refrigerator
fritto fried
frizione *f* clutch *(of car)*
fronte *f* forehead; **di fronte a**
 opposite *(prep)*
frutti *mpl* **di mare** seafood,
 shellfish
fruttivendolo *m* grocer's
frutto *m*: **un frutto** a piece of
 fruit
fumare to smoke
fumatore *m*, **fumatrice** *f*
 smoker
fumo *m* smoke
fuochi *mpl* **d'artificio** fireworks
fuoco m fire; **al fuoco!** fire!

fuori outside
furto *m* theft, rip-off
fusibile *m* fuse

G

galleria *f* gallery
Galles *m* Wales
gallese Welsh *(adj)*
gallese *m* Welsh *(language)*; **i**
 gallesi the Welsh *(people)*
gamba *f* leg
garanzia *f* guarantee
gas *m* gas
gasato fizzy
gastronomia *f* deli, delicatessen
gay gay
gel *m* **da doccia** shower gel
generale general
genitori *mpl* parents
gennaio *m* January
gente *f*: **la gente** people
Germania *f* Germany
gesso *m* plaster (cast)
ghiaccio *m* ice
già already
giallo yellow
giardino *m* garden
giardino *m* **botanico** botanical
 garden
ginecologo *m*, **ginecologa** *f*
 gynaecologist
ginocchio *m* knee
giocare to play
giocattolo *m* toy
gioielleria *f* jeweller's
gioielli *mpl* jewellery
giornalaio *m* newsagent
giornale *m* newspaper

giorno *m* day; **al giorno d'oggi** nowadays
giorno *m* **festivo** public holiday
giovane young
giovedì *m* Thursday
girare to turn
giro *m*: **fare un giro in macchina** to go for a drive
giugno *m* June
giusto right, correct, fair
gli *(def art)* the
gli *(pron)* him, to him, them, to them
gocce *fpl* drops *(for eyes)*
gola *f* throat
golf *m* golf, sweater
gomma *f* **a terra** flat tyre
gomma *f* **di scorta** spare tyre
gonfio swollen
gonna *f* skirt
gradino *m* step *(of stair)*
grado *m* degree
grammi *mpl* grams
Gran Bretagna *f* Great Britain
grande big
grande magazzino *m* department store
grasso fat *(adj)*
grattacielo *m* skyscraper
gratuito free *(for nothing)*
grazie thanks, thank you; **grazie mille** thank you very much; **grazie a** thanks to
Grecia *f* Greece
greco Greek *(adj)*
greco *m* Greek *(language)*
greco *m*, **greca** *f* Greek *(person)*
grigio grey
grigliata *f* barbecue

guanciale *m* pillow
guanto *m* **di spugna** facecloth
guardare to look at, to watch
guardaroba *m* cloakroom
guasto out of order *(not working)*
guasto *m* breakdown
guida *f* guide, guidebook
guidare to drive
gusto *m* taste, flavour

hashish *m* hashish

idraulico *m* plumber
ieri yesterday; **ieri sera** yesterday evening
il, la, i, le the; **le tre** three o'clock
imbarcarsi to board *(onto plane)*
imbarco *m* boarding *(onto plane)*
imbucare to post
immersione *f* scuba diving; **fare immersioni** to go diving
imparare to learn
impermeabile waterproof *(adj)*
impermeabile *m* raincoat
importante important
importare: non importa it doesn't matter
in in; **in Inghilterra** in England; **in italiano** in Italian; **nel 2006** in 2006; **nel diciannovesimo secolo** in the 19th century
incendio *m* fire
incidente *m* accident
incinta pregnant
incontrare to meet
indipendente independent
indirizzo *m* address

indirizzo m **e-mail** e-mail address
indossare to wear
infarto m heart attack
infermiere m, **infermiera** f nurse
infezione f infection
influenza f flu
influenza f **intestinale** gastric flu
informazioni fpl information
infradito mpl flip-flops
Inghilterra f England
inglese English (adj)
inglese m English (language); **gli
  inglesi** the English (people)
ingorgo m **stradale** traffic jam
ingresso m entrance, admission
iniezione f injection
iniziare to begin
inizio m beginning; **all'inizio** at
  the beginning
innanzitutto first (of all)
insetticida m insecticide
insetto m insect
insieme together
insolazione f sunstroke;
  prendere un'insolazione to get
  sunstroke
insonnia f insomnia
**intenzione: avere intenzione
  di …** to intend to …
internazionale international
Internet m Internet
Internet café m Internet café
intero whole (adj)
intorno a around (prep)
intossicazione f **alimentare**
  food poisoning
inutile useless
invece instead; **invece di** instead of
inverno m winter

inversione f **a U** U-turn
investire to knock down (with car)
invitare to invite
io I; **anch'io** me too
Irlanda f Ireland
irlandese Irish (adj)
irlandese m Irish (language); **gli
  irlandesi** the Irish (people)
isola f island
italiano Italian (adj)
italiano m Italian (language)
italiano m, **italiana** f Italian
  (person)
IVA f VAT

J

jetlag m jetlag
jogging m jogging

K

kayak m kayak
kilometro m kilometre

L

la (def art) the
la (pron) her, it
labbro m lip
ladro m, **ladra** f thief
lago m lake
lamentarsi to complain
lametta f **(da barba)** razor blade
lampada f lamp
lampadina f light bulb
lana f wool
largo wide
lasciare to let (allow)

lato *m* side

lattina *f* can *(for liquid)*

lavanderia *f* **(a secco)** dry cleaner's

lavanderia *f* **automatica** launderette

lavandino *m* washbasin

lavare to wash; **lavare i panni** to do the washing; **lavarsi i capelli** to wash one's hair

lavastoviglie *f* dishwasher

lavata: darsi una lavata to have a wash

lavatrice *f* washing machine

lavorare to work

lavori *mpl* **di casa** housework; **fare i lavori di casa** to do the housework

lavoro *m* work, job

le *(def art)* the

le *(pron)* her, to her

leggere to read

legno *m* wood *(material)*

lei she; **a lei** to her

lentamente slowly

lente *f* lens

lenti *fpl* **(a contatto)** (contact) lenses

lento slow

lenzuolo *m* sheet *(for bed)*

lettera *f* letter

letto *m* bed; **andare a letto con** to sleep with

li *(pron)* them

lì *(adv)* there, over there

libbra *f* pound

libero free

libreria *f* bookshop

libro *m* book

lieto: molto lieto! pleased to meet you!

light low-fat

linea *f* line

linea *f* **dell'autobus** bus route

linea *f* **della metropolitana** underground line

lingua *f* tongue *(in mouth)*; language

litro *m* litre

lo *(def art)* the

lo *(pron)* him, it

locale *m* **notturno** nightclub

località *f* **balneare** seaside resort

località *f* **sciistica** ski resort

lontano far; **lontano da** far from

loro they; **(a) loro** (to) them; **il loro, la loro, i loro, le loro** their, theirs

lottare to fight

luce *f* light

luglio *m* July

lui he; **a lui** to him

luna *f* moon

luna park *m* funfair

lunedì *m* Monday

lungo long

Lussemburgo *f* Luxembourg *(city)*

Lussemburgo *m* Luxembourg *(country)*

lusso *m* luxury *(n)*; **di lusso** luxury *(adj)*

ma but

macchia *f* stain

macchina *f* car; **in macchina** by car

macchina _f_ **fotografica** camera
macchina _f_ **fotografica digitale** digital camera
macelleria _f_ butcher's
madre _f_ mother
maggio _m_ May
maggiore: la maggior parte della gente most people
maglione _m_ jumper
magro thin
mai never
mal _m_ **di gola** sore throat; **avere mal di gola** to have a sore throat
mal _m_ **di mare** seasickness; **avere il mal di mare** to be seasick
mal _m_ **di pancia** stomachache; **avere mal di pancia** to have a stomachache
mal _m_ **di testa** headache; **avere mal di testa** to have a headache
malato ill
malattia _f_ illness
male: non è male it's not bad; **fa male** it hurts; **mi fa male la testa** my head hurts; **avere male alla testa** to have a sore head
mancare to miss; **mancano due ...** there are two ... missing; **mi mancano due ...** I'm two ... short
mancia _f_ tip _(gratuity)_
mangiare to eat
manica _f_ sleeve; **a maniche corte** short-sleeved
mano _f_ hand
mare _m_ sea; **al mare** at the seaside
marina _f_ marina

marito _m_ husband
marrone brown
martedì _m_ Tuesday
marzo _m_ March
materasso _m_ mattress
matita _f_ pencil
mattino _m_ morning
maturo ripe
me: a me to me
medicina _f_ medicine
medico _m_ doctor
medico _m_ **generico** GP
medio medium
meglio better; **è meglio ...** it's better to ...; **molto meglio** all the better
membro _m_ member
meno less; **meno di** less than
mento _m_ chin
mentre while _(conj)_
menu _m_ menu
meraviglioso wonderful
mercato _m_ market
merce _f_ goods
mercoledì _m_ Wednesday
mese _m_ month
messa _f_ mass _(religious service)_
messaggio _m_ message
mestruazioni _fpl_ period _(menstruation)_
metro _m_ metre
metro _f_ tube, underground
metropolitana _f_ tube, underground
mettere to put
mezzanotte _f_ midnight
mezza pensione _f_ half-board
mezzo half; **mezzo litro/kilo** half a litre/kilo

mezzo *m* middle; **in mezzo (a)** in the middle (of)

mezzogiorno *m* midday, noon

mezzora *f* half an hour

mi me, to me, myself, to myself

migliorare to get better

migliore better, best; **il (la) migliore** the best

minimo least

ministro *m* minister

minuto *m* minute; **all'ultimo minuto** at the last minute

mio: il mio, la mia, i miei, le mie my, mine

mittente *m* sender

moderno modern

modo *m* way; **in modo che** so that

moglie *f* wife

molti many; **molti turisti** many tourists, a lot of tourists

molto *(adj)* a lot of; **molto lavoro** a lot of work; **molto tempo** a long time

molto *(adv)* very, a lot; **è molto lontano?** is it very far?; **viaggia molto** she travels a lot

momento *m* moment

monastero *m* monastery

mondo *m* world

moneta *f* coin

montagna *f* mountain

monumento *m* monument

mordere to bite

morire to die

morso *m* bite

morto dead *(person)*

mosca *f* fly *(insect)*

moschea *f* mosque

mostra *f* exhibition

mostrare to show

moto(cicletta) *f* motorbike

motore *m* engine

motorino *m* moped

mountain bike *f* mountain bike

mouse *m* mouse *(for computer)*

mulino *m* mill

multa *f* fine

municipio *m* town hall

muscolo *m* muscle

museo *m* museum

musica *f* music

muta *f* wetsuit

mutande *fpl* pants

---

naso *m* nose

natura *f* nature

nausea *f*: **avere la nausea** to feel sick

navetta *f* shuttle

navigare to sail

né: né …, né … neither … nor …

necessario necessary

negoziante *mf* shopkeeper

negozio *m* shop

nemmeno: nemmeno io neither do I

nero black

nessuno *(adj)* no, not any; **non ho nessuna fretta** I'm in no hurry

nessuno *(pron)* nobody, none

neve *f* snow

nevicare to snow

niente nothing; **per niente** not at all; **non fa niente** that's OK

no no; **no, grazie** no, thank you
noi we; **a noi** to us
noleggiare to hire
noleggio *m* hire
nome *m* name
nome *m* **da ragazza** maiden name
nome *m* **(di battesimo)** first name
non not
non fumatori non-smoking
nonostante although
nord *m* north; **a nord** in the north; **a nord di** (to the) north of
nostro: il nostro, la nostra, i nostri, le nostre our, ours
nota *f* note
notizie *fpl* news
noto well-known
notte *f* night
novembre *m* November
nudo naked
numero *m* number
numero *m* **di targa** registration number
numero *m* **di telefono** phone number
nuotare to swim
nuotata: fare una nuotata to go for a swim
nuoto *m* swimming
nuovo new; **di nuovo** again

---

o

o or
occhiali *mpl* glasses
occhiali *mpl* **da sole** sunglasses
occhio *m* eye

occuparsi di to look after
occupato busy *(person)*; engaged *(toilet)*
oceano *m* ocean
odiare to hate
odore *m* smell; **avere un buon/cattivo odore** to smell good/bad
officina *f* garage
offrire to offer
oggi today
ogni each, every; **ogni giorno** every day
ognuno each one
Olanda *f* Holland
olio *m* oil
ombra *f* shade; **all'ombra** in the shade
ombrello *m* umbrella
ombrellone *m* beach umbrella
omosessuale homosexual
onda *f* wave
onesto honest
opera *f* **d'arte** work of art
operare to operate
operazione *f* operation; **subire un'operazione** to have an operation
opinione *f* opinion
opportunità *f* opportunity
ora now
ora *f* hour; **un'ora e mezza** an hour and a half; **che ore sono?** what time is it?
ora *f* **di chiusura** closing time
ora *f* **locale** local time
orario *m* timetable; **in orario** on time
orchestra *f* orchestra
ordinare to order

ordinato tidy
ordine m order
orecchini mpl earrings
orecchio m ear
organizzare to organize, to arrange
orgoglioso (di) proud (of)
orientamento m: **avere il senso dell'orientamento** to have a good sense of direction
orologio m watch (for telling time)
ospedale m hospital
ospitare to put up (guest)
ospite mf guest
ostello m **della gioventù** youth hostel
ottenere to get
ottico m optician
ottimo fine, great
ottobre m October
otturazione f filling (in tooth)
ovatta f cotton wool
ovest m west; **a ovest** in the west; **a ovest di** (to the) west of
ovvio obvious

P

pacchetto m packet, parcel
padella f frying pan
padre m father
paesaggio m scenery, landscape
paese m country, village
Paesi Bassi mpl Netherlands
pagare to pay; **far pagare** to charge (amount)
paio m pair; **un paio di pantaloni corti** a pair of shorts
palazzo m palace, building

pallavolo f volleyball
pallina f scoop (of ice cream); **una pallina/due palline** one/two scoop(s)
pane m bread
panetteria f baker's
pannolino m nappy
pantaloni mpl trousers
parabrezza m windscreen
paraurti m bumper
parcheggiare to park
parcheggio m car park
parco m park
parco m **a tema** theme park
parecchi several; **parecchie macchine** several cars, quite a lot of cars
parecchio quite a lot of; **parecchio tempo** quite a lot of time
parere: fai come ti pare! do as you please!
parlare to speak, to talk
parrucchiere m, **parrucchiera** f hairdresser
parte f part; **far parte di** to be a part of; **da qualche parte** somewhere; **da qualche altra parte** somewhere else; **da nessuna parte** nowhere
partenza f departure
partire to leave
partita f game, match
Pasqua f Easter
passaggio m: **dare un passaggio a qualcuno** to give someone a lift
passaporto m passport
passare to pass

passato past
passeggero m passenger
passeggiata f: **andare a fare una passeggiata** to go for a walk
passeggino m pushchair
pasto m meal
patente f **(di guida)** driving licence
patito m, **patita** f fan (person)
pattumiera f dustbin
paura f: **aver paura (di)** to be scared (of)
pavimento m floor
paziente mf patient
pc m **portatile** laptop
peccato! it's a pity!, too bad!
pedaggio m toll
pedone m pedestrian
peggio worse (adv)
peggiorare to get worse
peggiore worse (adj); **it's worse (than)** è peggiore (di)
pelle f skin
pellicola f film (for camera)
penna f pen
pensare to think
pensione f guest house
pensione f **completa** full board
pentola f pot (for cooking)
per for; **per un'ora** for an hour
perché why, because
perdere to lose; **perdersi** to get lost; **essersi perso** to be lost; **abbiamo perso il treno** we missed the train
perdita f leak
perfetto perfect
pericoloso dangerous
persiana f shutter (on window)

persona f person
pertanto therefore
pesante heavy
pesce m fish
pescheria f fishmonger's, fish shop
pettine m comb
petto m chest
pezzo m piece, bit; **un pezzo di** a piece of
piacere: piacere a to please; **mi piace** I like him; **mi piace ballare** I like dancing
piacere m pleasure
piangere to cry
piano m storey
pianta f plant
pianterreno m ground floor
piastra f **(di cottura)** hotplate
piatti mpl dishes; **lavare i piatti** to do the dishes
piatto m dish, plate
piatto m **da asporto** takeaway
piatto m **del giorno** dish of the day; **il piatto del giorno** today's special
piatto flat (adj)
piazza f square (in town)
piccante spicy
picchetto m tent peg
piccolo little, small
picnic m picnic; **fare un picnic** to have a picnic
piede m foot
pieno full; **pieno di** full of; **pieno di gente** packed
pieno m: **fare il pieno (di benzina)** to fill up with petrol
pietra f stone

pigiama m: **un pigiama** a pair of pyjamas

pillola f pill; **prendere la pillola** to be on the pill

pillola f **del giorno dopo** morning-after pill

pioggia f rain

piovere: piove it's raining

pipì f: **fare la pipì** to pee

piscina f swimming pool

pista f **ciclabile** cycle path

più more, most, the most; **più di** more than; **molto di più** much more, a lot more; **non c'è più …** there's no more …

piuttosto rather

placcato (d')argento silver-plated

plastica f plastic

pneumatico m tyre

pochi few

poco little; **un po'** a little; **un po' di** some; **un po' di pane** some bread

poi then

polizia f police

polmone m lung

polso m wrist

polvere f powder

pomata f ointment

pomeriggio m afternoon

pompa f **da bicicletta** bicycle pump

pompieri mpl fire brigade

ponte m bridge

porta f door

portabagagli m boot (of car)

portacenere m ashtray

portafoglio m wallet

portare to carry, to bring

porto m port

Portogallo m Portugal

portoghese Portuguese (adj)

portoghese m Portuguese (language); **i portoghesi** the Portuguese (people)

possedere to own

possibile possible

posta f post, mail

poster m poster

postino m postman

posto m place

posto m **(a sedere)** seat

posto m **(per la) macchina** parking space

postumi mpl **di una sbornia** hangover

potere can, to be able to; **non posso** I can't; **potrebbe piovere** it might rain

povero poor

pranzare to have lunch

pranzo m lunch

pratico practical

precedente previous

preferire to prefer

preferito favourite

prefisso m **(telefonico)** dialling code

prelevare to withdraw

premere to press

premio m prize

prendere to take, to catch; **andare a prendere qualcuno/ qualcosa** to go and fetch someone/something

prenotare to book, to reserve

prenotato booked, reserved

preparare to prepare;
  preparare la valigia to pack
  one's suitcase
presentare: ti presento … this
  is …
preservativo *m* condom
pressione *f* pressure
pressione *f* **sanguigna** blood
  pressure
pressione *f* **(sanguigna) alta**
  high blood pressure
pressione *f* **(sanguigna) bassa**
  low blood pressure
prestare to lend
prestito *m*: **prendere in
  prestito** to borrow
presto early, soon; **a presto!** see
  you soon!
previsioni *fpl* **(del tempo)**
  (weather) forecast
prezzo *m* price
prezzo *m* **pieno** full price
prima before *(adv)* ; **poco prima**
  just before; **il prima possibile** as
  soon as possible
prima classe *f* first class
prima colazione *f* breakfast
primavera *f* spring
primo *(adj)* first; *(n)* first course
primo piano *m* first floor
principale main
principiante *mf* beginner
privato private
probabilmente probably
problema *m* problem
prodotto *m* product
professione *f* profession
profondo deep
profumo *m* perfume

programma *m* plan, programme
promettere to promise
pronto *(adj)* ready
pronto! hello! *(on telephone)*
proporre to propose
proprietario *m*, **proprietaria**
  f owner
proprio *(adj)* own
proprio *(adv)* right; **proprio
  accanto a** right beside
prossimo next
proteggere to protect
provare to try, to try on; **provare
  a fare qualcosa** to try to do
  something
prudere: mi prude it's itchy
pubblico public
pulire to clean
pulito clean
pullman *m* coach *(bus)*
pungere to sting; **essere punto
  (da)** to get stung (by)
punto *m* point
punto *m* **di riferimento**
  landmark
puntura *f* sting

qualcosa something;
  qualcos'altro something else
qualcuno somebody, someone
quale which
qualità *f* quality; **of good/bad
  quality** di buona/cattiva qualità
qualsiasi: qualsiasi cosa anything
quando when
quanti? how many?; **quante
  volte …?** how many times …?

quanto? how much?; **quanto costa?** how much is it?, how much does it cost?; **quanto (tempo) …?** how long … ?
quartiere m **periferico** suburb
quarto m quarter; **un quarto d'ora** a quarter of an hour; **le dieci meno un quarto** a quarter to ten; **le dieci e un quarto** a quarter past ten
quasi almost
quelli those; **quelli (lì)** those ones
quello that; **quello (lì)** that one
questi these; **questi (qui)** these ones
questo this; **questo (qui)** this one
qui here

racchetta f racket
racchetta f **da sci** ski pole
raccomandato registered (letter)
radiatore m radiator (in car)
radio f radio
radiografia f X-ray
rado: di rado seldom
raffreddore m cold; **avere il raffreddore** to have a cold
raffreddore m **da fieno** hay fever
ragazza f girl, girlfriend
raggiungere to reach
ragionevole reasonable
ragno m spider
rapido fast
raramente rarely
raro rare
rasoio m razor

rasoio m **elettrico** electric shaver
rassegna f **delle manifestazioni** listings magazine
razzista mf racist
realtà f: **in realtà** in fact
reception f reception; **alla reception** at reception
receptionist mf receptionist
regalo m present (gift)
reggiseno m bra
Regno Unito m United Kingdom
rene m kidney
reparto m department
restituire to give back
resto m change (money); **il resto** the rest
retromarcia f reverse gear
reumatismi mpl rheumatism
riaprire to reopen
ricambio m: **(pezzo** m **di) ricambio** spare part
ricerca f **elenco abbonati** directory enquiries
ricetta f recipe
ricevere to receive
ricevuta f receipt
richiamare to call back
riconoscere to recognize
ricordare to remember, to remind
ridere to laugh
ridurre to reduce
riduzione reduction
riempire to fill
rifiutare to refuse
riflettere: riflettere su to think about
rifugio m **(di montagna)** mountain hut

rimanere to stay; **rimanere in contatto** to stay in touch; **rimanere calmo** to keep calm; **rimanere senza benzina** to run out of petrol; **rimanga in linea!** hold on! *(on the phone)*
rimborsare to refund
rimborso *m* refund; **ottenere un rimborso** to get a refund
ringraziare to thank
riparare to repair; **far riparare qualcosa** to get something repaired
ripetere to repeat
riposarsi to rest
risalire: risalire a to date from
riscaldamento *m* heating
rischio *m* risk
risparmiare to save *(money)*
rispondere to answer
risposta *f* answer
ristorante *m* restaurant
ritardo *m* delay; **in ritardo** delayed
ritornare to come back
ritorno *m* return
ritratto *f* portrait
riunione *f* meeting
riuscire: riuscire a fare qualcosa to manage to do something
rivista *f* magazine
roccia *f* rock
Rollerblade® *mpl* rollerblades
romanzo *m* novel
rompere to break; **rompersi** to break down; **rompersi una gamba** to break one's leg
rosa pink

rosso red
rosso *m* red light *(traffic light)*
rotatoria *f* roundabout
rotondo round *(adj)*
rotto broken
roulotte *f* caravan
rovinare to spoil
rovine *fpl* ruins; **in rovina** in ruins
rubare to steal
rubinetto *m* tap
rubinetto *m* **(di arresto)** stopcock
rumore *m* noise; **fare un rumore** to make a noise
rumoroso noisy
ruota *f* wheel
ruota *f* **di scorta** spare wheel

S

sabato *m* Saturday
sabbia *f* sand
sacchetto *m* **di plastica** plastic bag
sacco *m* **a pelo** sleeping bag
sala *f* **concerti** concert hall
salato salty, salted
saldi *mpl* sales
saldo *m*: **in saldo** in the sales
sale *m* salt
salute *f* health; **salute!** bless you! *(after sneeze)*
salve! hello!
sandali *mpl* sandals
sangue *m* blood; **al sangue** rare *(meat)*
sanguinare to bleed
sapere to know; **non lo so** I don't know

sapone m soap

sbagliarsi to be wrong

sbagliato wrong

sbrigarsi to hurry (up)

sbucciare to peel

scaldabagno m water heater

scale fpl stairs

scarafaggio m cockroach

scarico dead (battery)

scarpe fpl **da tennis** tennis shoes

scarpe fpl shoes

scarponi mpl boots (for hiking)

scarponi mpl **da montagna**
  walking boots

scatola f tin, can (for food)

scatola f **del cambio** gearbox

scendere to get off (from bus,
  train)

scheda f **telefonica** phonecard

scheggia f splinter

schiena f back (of body)

schiuma f **da barba** shaving foam

sci m skiing, ski

sci m **acquatico** waterskiing

sciare to ski; **andare a sciare** to
  go skiing

scioccante shocking

sciroppo m syrup

scodella f bowl

scogliera f cliff

scomodo uncomfortable

scompartimento m
  compartment

sconto m discount, concession;
  fare uno sconto a qualcuno to
  give someone a discount

scontrino m receipt (from shop)

scooter m scooter

scoppiare to burst

scoppiato burst (adj)

scorciatoia f short cut

scorso last; **l'anno scorso** last
  year

scotch m scotch (whisky)

Scotch® m Sellotape®

scottarsi: scottarsi al sole to get
  sunburnt

Scozia f Scotland

scozzese (adj) Scottish

scozzese mf Scot

scrivere to write, to spell; **come
  si scrive?** how do you spell it?

scuola f school

scuola f **secondaria** secondary
  school

scuro dark; **blu scuro** dark blue

scusa f excuse

scusare: scusi! sorry!; **mi scusi**
  excuse me; **(mi) scusi?** pardon?

se if

sé himself, herself, itself, themselves

secolo m century

seconda classe f second class

secondo (adj) second; **di
  seconda mano** second-hand

secondo (prep): **secondo me** in
  my opinion

secondo m main course

sedersi to sit down

sedia f chair

sedia f **a rotelle** wheelchair

seggiovia f chairlift

segnale m signal

segreteria f **telefonica** answering
  machine

selvaggio wild

semaforo m **rosso** red light
  (traffic light)

sembrare to seem, to look; **sembra che …** it seems that …

sempre always; **sempre dritto** straight ahead, straight on

sensazione f feeling (physical)

sensibile sensitive

senso m sense

sentiero m path

sentimento m feeling (emotional)

sentire to feel, to hear; **sentirsi bene/male** to feel good/bad; **sentire odore di qualcosa** to smell something

senza without; **senza glutine** gluten-free

separarsi to split up (couple)

separatamente separately

separato separate

sera f evening; **di sera** in the evening

serio serious

servire: servire a to be used for

sesso m sex

sete f thirst; **avere sete** to be thirsty

settembre m September

settimana f week

sfinito exhausted

shampoo m shampoo

shock m shock

si himself, to himself, herself, to herself, itself, to itself, themselves, to themselves

sì yes

sicurezza f security, safety

sicuro secure, safe, sure

sigaretta f cigarette

sigaro m cigar

signor Mr

signora Mrs, Ms

signorina Miss, Ms

silenzioso silent, quiet

simpatico nice (person)

sinagoga f synagogue

single single

sinistra f left; **a sinistra (di)** to the left (of)

sinistro left (adj)

sistemazione f accommodation

sito m **web** website

ski-lift m ski lift

slogarsi: slogarsi la caviglia to sprain one's ankle

smettere: smettere di fare qualcosa to stop doing something

soccorso m **stradale** breakdown service

società f company (business)

soffrire (di) to suffer (from)

soggiorno m stay, living room

soldi mpl money

sole m sun; **al sole** in the sun; **prendere il sole** to sunbathe

solito: di solito usually

solo only, just; **solo un po'** just a little; **solo uno** just one

somigliare: somigliare a to look like

sonnellino m nap; **fare un sonnellino** to have a nap

sonnifero m sleeping pill

sonno m sleep; **avere sonno** to be sleepy

sopportare to put up with

sopra above; **di sopra** upstairs

sordo deaf

sorella f sister

sorprendere to surprise

sorpresa *f* surprise
sorridere to smile
sorriso *m* smile
sotto *(prep)* under, below
sotto *(adv)* underneath; **di sotto** downstairs
sottotitolato subtitled
souvenir *m* souvenir
Spagna *f* Spain
spagnolo Spanish *(adj)*
spagnolo *m* Spanish *(language)*; **gli spagnoli** the Spanish *(people)*
spalla *f* shoulder
spazzatura *f* rubbish; **portare fuori la spazzatura** to take the rubbish out
spazzola *f* brush
spazzolino *m* **da denti** toothbrush
specchio *m* mirror
speciale special
specialità *f* speciality
spedire to send
spegnere to switch off, to put out
spendere to spend
spesa *f*: **fare la spesa** to do the shopping
spesso often
spettacolo *m* show
spettacolo *m* **teatrale** play *(in theatre)*
spezia *f* spice
spiaggia *f* beach
spina *f* plug *(electrical)*
spingere to push
spirale *f* coil *(contraceptive)*
spogliatoio *m* changing room *(at swimming pool, gym)*
sporco dirty

sport *m* sport
sportivo sporty
sposato married
sprecare to waste
spugna *f* sponge
spuntino *m*: **fare uno spuntino** to have a snack
squadra *f* team
stadio *m* stadium
stagione *f* season
stagnola *f* tinfoil
stanco tired
stanotte tonight
stanza *f* room
stare: stare per fare to be about to do
stasera this evening, tonight
Stati Uniti *mpl* United States
stato *m* state
stazione *f* station
stazione *f* **degli autobus** bus station
stazione *f* **della metro** tube station, underground station
stazione *f* **della metropolitana** tube station, underground station
stazione *f* **di servizio** petrol station
stazione *f* **ferroviaria** train station
stazione *f* **radiofonica** radio station
stereo *m* hi-fi
stesso same; **lo stesso** the same; **per me è lo stesso** I don't mind
stile *m* style
stirare to iron
stitico constipated
stivale *m* boot *(knee-length)*
stoffa *f* material

stomaco *m* stomach

strada *f* street, road

strada *f* **pedonale** pedestrianized street

straniero foreign

straniero *m*, **straniera** *f* foreigner

strano strange

stretto tight

strofinaccio *m* **da cucina** dish towel

studente *m*, **studentessa** *f* student

studi *mpl* studies

studiare to study; **studiare biologia** to study biology

stufo (di) fed up (with)

stupro *m* rape

su on

subito right away

succedere to happen

succo *m* juice

sud *m* south; **a sud** in the south; **a sud di** (to) south of

sudare to sweat

sudore *m* sweat

suggerire to suggest

suo: il suo, la sua, i suoi, le sue his, her, its *(adj)*; his, hers, its *(pron)*

super: (benzina) super *f* four-star petrol

superare: i miei bagagli superano il peso consentito my luggage is overweight

superato out of date

supermercato *m* supermarket

supplemento *m* supplement

surf *m* surfing, surfboard; **fare surf** to surf, to go surfing

sveglia *f* alarm clock

svegliarsi to wake up

svenimento *m* blackout *(fainting)*

svenire to faint

sviluppare: far sviluppare un rullino to get a film developed

T

tabaccheria *f* tobacconist's

tabacco *m* tobacco

taccuino *m* notebook

taglia *f* size

tagliare to cut; **tagliarsi** to cut oneself

tanto: di tanto in tanto from time to time

tappeto *m* rug

tappi *mpl* **per le orecchie** earplugs

tardi late

tariffa *f* fare

tariffa *f* **intera** full fare

tassa *f* tax

tassista *mf* taxi driver

tasso *m* **di cambio** exchange rate

tavolo *m* table

taxi *m* taxi

tazza *f* cup

te: a te to you *(singular)*

teatro *m* theatre

tedesco German *(adj)*

tedesco *m* German *(language)*

tedesco *m*, **tedesca** *f* German *(person)*

tegame *m* saucepan

telefonare to telephone, to phone

telefonata *f* phone call; **fare una telefonata** to make a phone call

telefono *m* telephone, phone
televisione *f* television
telo *m* **impermeabile (da mettere per terra)** ground sheet
temperatura *f* temperature
tempia *f* temple *(on head)*
tempo *m* time, weather; **è brutto tempo** the weather's bad
temporale *m* storm
temporaneo temporary
tenda *f* tent
tenere to hold, to keep
tennis *m* tennis
terminale *m* terminal
termometro *m* thermometer
termosifone *m* radiator *(in room)*
terra *f* earth, ground; **per terra** on the ground, on the floor
terrazza *f* terrace
terreno *m* **sportivo** sports ground
terribile terrible
tessera *f* card
tesserino *m* pass *(for public transport)*
testa *f* head
thermos *m* (Thermos®) flask
ti you, to you, yourself, to yourself
tiepido lukewarm
tipico typical
tipo *m* kind, type; **che tipo di …?** what kind of …?
tirare to pull, to throw
toccare to touch; **tocca a te** it's your turn
togliere to remove
toilette *f* toilet
topo *m* mouse *(animal)*

torcia *f* **elettrica** torch
torta *f* pie
tosse *f* cough; **avere la tosse** to have a cough
tossire to cough
tovagliolo *m* napkin
tovagliolo *m* **di carta** paper napkin
tra among; **tra un'ora** in an hour
tradizionale traditional
tradurre to translate
traffico *m* traffic
traghetto *m* ferry
tram *m* tram
tramonto *m* sunset
tranne except
trappola *f* **per turisti** tourist trap
traveller's cheque *m* traveller's cheque
treno *m* train; **il treno per Firenze** the train to Florence
triste sad
troppi *(adj)* too many; **troppi turisti** too many tourists
troppo *(adj)* too much; **troppo sale** too much salt
troppo *(adv)* too; **troppo tardi** too late
trovare to find
tu you *(singular, subject)*
tubo *m* **di scappamento** exhaust (pipe)
tuffarsi to dive
tuo: il tuo, la tua, i tuoi, le tue your *(singular)*, yours *(singular)*
turista *mf* tourist
tutti everybody, everyone; **tutti e due** both

tutto all; **tutto il giorno** all day; **tutta la settimana** all week; **tutto il tempo** all the time; **tutto compreso** all inclusive; **tutta la torta** the whole cake

U

ubriaco drunk
uccidere to kill
ufficio *m* **postale** post office
ufficio *m* **turistico** tourist office
ultimo last *(adj)*
umido damp
umore *m*: **essere di buon/cattivo umore** to be in a good/bad mood
una *f*: **l'una** one o'clock
unghia *f* nail *(on finger, toe)*
un(o), una a
uno one
uomo *m* man
urgente urgent
usa e getta disposable
usare to use
uscire to go out, to come out
uscita *f* exit, way out; gate *(at airport)*
uscita *f* **di sicurezza** emergency exit
utile useful

V

vacanza *f* holiday; **in vacanza** on holiday
vaccinato (contro) vaccinated (against)
vaglia *m* **internazionale** international money order

valere to be worth; **ne vale la pena** it's worth it
valido (per) valid (for)
valigia *f* suitcase
valle *f* valley
valuta *f* currency
vasetto *m* pot *(of yoghurt)*
vecchio old
vedere to see
vegetariano vegetarian
vela *f* sailing; **fare vela** to go sailing
veloce quick
velocemente quickly
velocità *f* speed; **a tutta velocità** at full speed
vendere to sell
vendita *f*: **in vendita** for sale
venerdì *m* Friday
venire to come
ventilatore *m* fan *(electric)*
vento *m* wind
verde green
vergogna *f* shame
verificare to check
vero true
verso towards
vescica *f* blister
vespa *f* wasp
vestirsi to get dressed
vetrate *fpl* stained-glass windows
vetrina *f*: **in vetrina** in the window
vi you, to you, yourselves, to yourselves
via *f* street
via aerea airmail
viaggiare to travel

viaggio *m* journey, trip; **buon viaggio!** have a good trip!

viaggio *m* **di andata** outward journey

viaggio *m* **di nozze** honeymoon

viaggio *m* **organizzato** package holiday

viale *m* avenue

vicino near; **il … più vicino** the nearest …; **vicino alla spiaggia** near the beach

vicino *m*, **vicina** *f* neighbour

vietato forbidden

villa *f* villa

villaggio *m* **turistico** holiday camp

vino *m* wine

vino *m* **bianco** white wine

vino *m* **rosato** rosé wine

vino *m* **rosso** red wine

viola purple

visita *f* visit

visita *f* **guidata** guided tour

visitare to visit

vista *f* view

vista *f* **sul mare** sea view

visto *m* visa

vita *f* life, waist

vivere to live

vivo alive

voi you *(plural, subject)*; **a voi** to you

voile *f* gauze

volantino *m* leaflet

volare to fly

volere to want; **voler fare qualcosa** to want to do something; **vorrei …** I'd like …; **voler dire** to mean; **cosa vuol dire …?** what does … mean?; **ci vogliono due ore** it takes 2 hours

volo *m* flight

volta *f* time *(occasion)*; **a volte** sometimes; **una volta** once; **una volta al giorno/all'ora** once a day/an hour; **due volte** twice; **tre/quattro volte** three/four times

vomitare to vomit

vostro: il vostro, la vostra, i vostri, le vostre your *(plural)*, yours *(plural)*

vuoto empty

WZ

Walkman® *m* Walkman®, personal stereo

windsurf *m* windsurfing

zaino *m* backpack, rucksack

zanzara *f* mosquito

zero *m* zero

zia *f* aunt

zio *m* uncle

zona *f* area; **in zona** in the area

zoo *m* zoo

zoom *m* zoom (lens)

GRAMMAR

The articles

masculine

definite		indefinite	
singular	*plural*	*singular*	*plural*
il libro the book	**i** libri the books	**un** museo a museum	**dei** musei some museums
lo zio the uncle (before z, s + consonant, ps, gn, or x)	**gli** zii the uncles	**uno** sconto a discount	**degli** sconti some discounts
l'albero the tree (before vowel)	**gli** alberi the trees	**un** uccello a bird	**degli** uccelli some birds

feminine

definite		indefinite	
singular	*plural*	*singular*	*plural*
la casa the house	**le** case the houses	**una** camera a bedroom	**delle** camere some bedrooms
l'arancia the orange (before vowel)	**le** arance the oranges	**un'**oliva an olive	**delle** olive some olives

Most nouns and adjectives ending in **o** are masculine, while most ending in **a** are feminine. As a general rule, the **plural of nouns and adjectives** is formed by replacing **o** by **i** and **a** by **e** : l'albero → gli alberi, la camera → le camere.

There are some exceptions :

- some nouns ending in **e** are masculine, while others are feminine, but they always form their plural with **i** : il fiore → i fiori (the flowers), **la** chiave → le chiavi (the keys).

- some nouns are masculine in the singular, but feminine in the plural:
  l'uovo → le uova (the eggs), il dito → le dita (the fingers), il labbro → le labbra (the lips), il braccio → le braccia (the arms).
- irregular plurals : l'uomo → gli uomini (the men), l'ala → le ali (the wings), la mano → le mani (the hands).

Some **prepositions** combine with the definite article as follows :

	il	lo	la	l'	i	gli	le
a	al	allo	alla	all'	ai	agli	alle
da	dal	dallo	dalla	dall'	dai	dagli	dalle
di	del	dello	della	dell'	dei	degli	delle
in	nel	nello	nella	nell'	nei	negli	nelle
su	sul	sullo	sulla	sull'	sui	sugli	sulle

N.B. It is important to distinguish between the prepositions **da** and **di**: da means 'from' or 'by' and di means 'of':

dalla finestra della mia camera from the window of my room

Possessive Adjectives and Pronouns

il mio	i miei	la mia	le mie
il tuo	i tuoi	la tua	le tue
il suo	i suoi	la sua	le sue
il nostro	i nostri	la nostra	le nostre
il vostro	i vostri	la vostra	le vostre
il loro	i loro	la loro	le loro

Possessive adjectives and pronouns are always preceded by the definite article, except when used with singular nouns referring to family members. The only exception to this rule is **loro**, which is always preceded by the definite article.

mio padre	my father
i miei genitori	my parents
il loro fratello	their brother

The definite article is also dropped after the verb **essere** 'to be' when there is no noun following:

questo libro è mio   this book is mine

The **demonstrative** adjectives and pronouns **questo** and **quello** agree like adjectives in gender and number with the nouns they refer to. Questo, meaning 'this', is used to indicate something close in space or time, whereas **quello**, meaning 'that', is used to indicate something more distant.

Personal Pronouns

subject	direct object	indirect object
io I	**me, mi** me	**mi** to me
tu you	**te, ti** you	**ti** to you
lei you	**lei, la** you	**le** to you
lui he, it	**lui, lo** him, it	**gli** to him, to it
lei she, it	**lei, la** her, it	**le** to her, to it
noi we	**noi, ci** us	**ci** to us
voi you	**voi, vi** you	**vi** to you
loro they	**loro, li** them	**loro** to them

NB The pronoun **lei** is used with a verb in the third person as a polite way of saying 'you' when talking to a stranger or someone you do not know well.

The **reflexive pronouns** are:

mi myself
ti yourself
si himself, herself, itself,
  yourself

ci ourselves
vi yourselves
si themselves, yourselves

Most of the time in Italian the form of the verb itself shows who is its subject, so that you only use a personal pronoun as the subject of a verb when you need to make it clear who you are talking about:

lui parla forte, **lei** parla piano   he speaks loudly, but she speaks softly

With the exception of **loro**, personal pronouns come in front of the verb when they are used as direct or indirect objects:

gli ho telefonato   I phoned him
come **si** chiama ?   what's your name?
ho dato **loro** il mio indirizzo   I gave them my address

With an infinitive or imperative, however, you attach direct or indirect personal pronouns to the end of the infinitive or imperative, and the infinitive drops its final **-e**:

sono andato a prender**li**	I went to fetch them
ascolta**mi**!	listen to me!

Ci and **vi** are also **adverbs** meaning 'there':

ci/vi vado spesso	I often go there

The particle **ne** is used to mean 'of it' or 'of them', or 'about it' or about them':

ne comprerò un chilo	I'll take a kilo of them
ne abbiamo parlato	we talked about it

Verbs fall in to one of three groups according to whether their infinitives end in -are, -ere or –ire.

Present

amare to love	**vendere** to sell	**partire** to leave
am**o**	vend**o**	part**o**
am**i**	vend**i**	part**i**
am**a**	vend**e**	part**e**
am**iamo**	vend**iamo**	part**iamo**
am**ate**	vend**ete**	part**ite**
am**ano**	vend**ono**	part**ono**

Perfect

ho am**ato**	ho vend**uto**	sono part**ito**
hai am**ato**	hai vend**uto**	sei part**ito**
ha am**ato**	ha vend**uto**	è part**ito**
abbiamo am**ato**	abbiamo vend**uto**	siamo part**iti**
avete am**ato**	avete vend**uto**	siete part**iti**
hanno am**ato**	hanno vend**uto**	sono part**iti**

Future

amerò	venderò	partirò
amerai	venderai	partirai
amerà	venderà	partirà
ameremo	venderemo	partiremo
amerete	venderete	partirete
ameranno	venderanno	partiranno

Auxiliary verbs

essere to be	**avere** to have
sono	ho
sei	hai
è	ha
siamo	abbiamo
siete	avete
sono	hanno

Some irregular past participles:

essere	stato	to be
aprire	aperto	to open
chiudere	chiuso	to close
mettere	messo	to put
nascere	nato	to be born
prendere	preso	to take
scendere	sceso	to go down
scrivere	scritto	to write
vedere	visto	to see
venire	venuto	to come

Some verbs are irregular in the present tense:

fare to do, make	**bere** to drink	**dire** to say
faccio	bevo	dico
fai	bevi	dici
fa	beve	dice
facciamo	beviamo	diciamo
fate	bevete	dite
fanno	bevono	dicono

andare to go	**venire** to come	**potere** to be able
vado	vengo	posso
vai	vieni	puoi
va	viene	può
andiamo	veniamo	possiamo
andate	venite	potete
vanno	vengono	possono

To make a sentence **negative**, you put **non** in front of the verb: **ho fame** I'm hungry; **non ho fame** I'm not hungry.

Only intonation (in speaking) and punctuation (in writing) show the difference between a **question** and a statement:

guardi il quadro	you are looking at the picture
guardi il quadro?	are you looking at the picture?

HOLIDAYS AND FESTIVALS

NATIONAL BANK HOLIDAYS

Bank holidays are called **giorni festivi** and working days are **giorni feriali**. On bank holidays, government offices and banks are closed, as well as most museums, shops and offices. Below is a list of national holidays in Italy, but note that local holidays also exist.

1 January	**capodanno** (New Year's Day)
6 January	**Epifania (la festa della Befana)** (Epiphany)
March/April	**Pasqua** (Easter Sunday)
	lunedì di Pasqua (Pasquetta) (Easter Monday)
25 April	**festa della Liberazione** (celebration of Italy's liberation from the Nazis in 1945)
1 May	**festa del Lavoro** (Labour Day)
2 June	**festa della Repubblica** (anniversary of the founding of the Italian Republic)
15 August	**Assunzione (Ferragosto)** (Assumption)
1 November	**Ognissanti** (All Saints Day)
8 December	**Immacolata Concezione** (Immaculate Conception)
25 December	**Natale** (Christmas Day)
26 December	**Santo Stefano** (St Stephen's Day, Boxing Day)

FESTIVALS AND CELEBRATIONS

Italy has a large number of traditional festivals, many of which date back to ancient times. Below are some of the best known, but most Italian towns also organize beautiful processions in honour of their patron saint and at Easter (Holy Week).

February	Several Italian towns celebrate **il Carnevale**. The best known carnivals are held in Venice and Viareggio.
15 May	**la festa dei ceri** (the festival of the candles of Gubbio). The streets of Gubbio, near Perugia in Umbria, are lined with candles and three teams carry

	enormous candles and the statues of three patron saints.
2 July, 16 August	The **Palio** in Siena in Tuscany. Horse races in medieval costume are held on the piazza del Campo.
1st Sunday in Sept.	The **Regata storica** (historical regatta) in Venice. A fancy-dress boat race is held on the Grand Canal.
September	The **partita di scacchi di Marostica** in the town square of Marostica, a small town near Vicenza in the Veneto. Games of chess are held featuring local people in medieval costume as the pieces.

Italians love fireworks (**fuochi d'artificio**), and here are some of the most impressive displays:

New Year's Eve	In Naples, fireworks are let off over the Piazza Plebiscito and can be seen and heard all over the city.
21 April	In Rome, the Aventine Hill is lit up to celebrate the founding of the city (in 753 BC).
3rd Saturday in July	In Venice, on the night of the **festa del Redentore**, the waterways sparkle with thousands of lights. Locals celebrate by sailing into Saint Mark's basin in decorated boats to admire the display.

USEFUL ADDRESSES

IN UK:

Italian State Tourist Board (ENIT)
1 Princes Street, London W1B 2AY
Telephone: 020 7408 1254
Fax: 020 7399 3567
italy@italiantouristboard.co.uk

IN ITALY:

Florence
British Consulate
Lungarno Corsini 2, 50123 Firenze
Telephone: (0039) 055 284133

Italian Tourist Office
Via Cavour 1r
Telephone: (0039) 055 290832

Milan
British Consulate General
Via S. Paolo 7, 20121 Milano
Telephone: (0039) 02 723001

Italian Tourist Office
Via Marconi 1
Telephone: (0039) 02 72524301

Naples
British Consulate
Via dei Mille 40, 80121 Napoli
Telephone: (0039) 081 423 8911

Italian Tourist Office
Piazza dei Martiri 58
Telephone: (0039) 081 410 7211

Rome
British Embassy
Via XX Settembre 80, 00187 Roma
Telephone: (0039) 06 4220 0001

Italian Tourist Office
Via Parigi 11
Telephone: (0039) 06 488 991

Venice
British Consulate
Piazzale Donatori di Sangue 2/5, 30171 Venezia-Mestre
Telephone: (0039) 041 5055990

Itallan Tourist Office
Castello 5050
Telephone: (0039) 041 5298700

Carabinieri (military police): 112
Police: 113
Fire Brigade : 115
Emergency Breakdown Service: 116
Ambulance : 118
Directory Enquiries: 412

CONVERSION TABLES

N.B. In decimals in Italian you use a comma where we use a decimal point in English. For example 0.6 would be written 0,6 in Italian.

Weight and Measurements

Italians only use the metric system. Below are the main British Imperial weights and measures with their metric equivalents.

Length and Distance

1 inch (pollice) ≈ 2.5 cm	1 yard (iarda) ≈ 90 cm
1 foot (piede) ≈ 30 cm	1 mile (miglio) ≈ 1.6 km

To convert miles into kilometres, divide by 5 and then multiply by 8.

kilometres	1	2	5	10	20	100
miles	0.6	3.2	8	16	32	160

To convert kilometres into miles, divide by 8 and then multiply by 5.

miles	1	2	5	10	20	100
kilometers	0.6	1.25	3.1	6.25	12.50	62.50

Weight
1 oz (oncia) ≈ 28.35 g   1 lb (libbra) ≈ 1/2 kg (454 g)
1 stone ≈ 6 kg
Abbreviations: **oz** = ounce (**oncia**) and **lb** = pound (**libbra**)

To convert kilos into pounds, divide by 5 and then multiply by 11.
To convert pounds into kilos, multiply by 5 and then divide by 11.

kilos	1	2	10	20	60	80
pounds	2.2	4.4	22	44	132	176

Capacity

1 pint (**pinta**) ≈ 1/2 **litro** (*Br* 0.57 **litro**, *Am* 0.47 **litro**)
1 gallon ≈ (*Br*) 4.54 **litri**, (*Am*) 3.78 **litri**

Temperature

To convert degrees Fahrenheit into degrees Celsius, subtract 32, multiply by 5 and then divide by 9.
To convert degrees Celsius into degrees Fahrenheit, divide by 5, multiply by 9 and then add 32.

Fahrenheit (°F)	32	40	50	59	68	86	100
Celsius (°C)	0	4	10	15	20	30	38

Clothes sizes

The abbreviations **XS** (Extra Small), **S** (Small), **M** (Medium), **L** (Large) and **XL** (Extra Large) are also used in Italy.

• Women's clothing

Br	8	10	12	14	16	etc
Am	6	8	10	12	14	
Italy	40	42	44	46	48	

• Bras (cup sizes are the same)

Br/Am	32	34	36	38	40	etc
Italy	1	2	3	4	5	

• Men's collar sizes

Br/Am	14	15	16	17	etc
Italy	36	38	41	43	

• Men's clothing

Br/Am	30	32	34	36	38	40	etc
Italy	40	42	44	46	48	50	

Shoe sizes

• Women's shoes

UK	4	5	6	7	8	etc
Am	6	7	8	9	10	
Italy	37	38	39	40	42	

• Men's shoes

UK	7	8	9	10	11	etc
Am	8	9	10	11	12	
Italy	40	42	43	44	46	